inside

Radical Loving Care

The Power of *The Mother Test*

Erie Chapman

PUBLISHED BY WESTVIEW, INC.
KINGSTON SPRINGS, TENNESSEE

PUBLISHED BY WESTVIEW, INC.
P.O. Box 605
Kingston Springs, TN 37082
www.publishedbywestview.com

ISBN 978-1-937763-95-4

First edition, May 2013

Cover photograph by Tia Ann Chapman, courtesy *The Hartford Courant*.

Parts of this text were originally included in Erie Chapman's two previous
works: *Radical Loving Care* and *Sacred Work*.

Printed in the United States of America on acid free paper.

iRLC

11. Loving Leadership 75

12. Further Strategies and Tools 87

About the Author 92

Introduction

During their stay in this world, artists feel compelled to express their experience of this earth. When you see Liz Wessel's art in the *Journal of Sacred Work* you know that she has applied her gifts to share something that will touch our hearts.

When you hear an aria from *Madame Butterfly*, you know that Puccini expressed something so exquisite that it thrills us to this day. When you see the one surviving photo of Emily Dickinson, you sense a gentle woman. Her poetry reflects a rich spirit both gentle and strong.

When the hybrid Stargazer lily appeared recently on this earth in 1974, lily-breeder Leslie Woodriff named her oriental combination "Stargazer" because of the way the new flower faced the sky.

The scent of the Stargazer changes us. It shows how flowers—their sight, scent and touch—can perfume your soul providing crucial relief, especially if your work immerses you in blood.

In music, photographs, film and poetry—even flowers—we can share together things we may encounter separately. Amid the brutality of the world that stains this spring we can open our hearts to gentle things.

Only Beauty's strength, both hard and soft, can heal a heart scarred by caregiving.

Caregivers, particularly male executives, sometimes ask me what Beauty has to do with medical care. I say that Beauty heals because it is Love's expression. They often shake their head, perhaps wondering how you heal a broken leg with a plant.

You know better.

For the first seven years of my career I was a trial lawyer—first handling auto accidents and worker's compensation claims and the last three years as a federal prosecutor. After that I worked eight more years as a part time night court judge while running a hospital.

Whether it is the setting for a divorce, a criminal prosecution, or the resolution of a malpractice case, courtrooms host ugliness. When I entered the caregiving world (the year after the first Stargazer bloomed) I naively imagined a world populated with kind souls ministering to the sick and wounded. I had not thought enough about the blood, the torn bodies, the horror that inhabits hospitals.

Over the next thirty years I saw more violence in hospitals than I had ever seen in courtrooms. Some was unexpected—especially in my role as a CEO removed from direct caregiving.

For example, on December 30, 1983, I was the third person on the scene (after the criminal and a doctor) to see the lifeless body of research technician Joyce McFadden lying on the floor of our hospital's research laboratory. She was bound up. Fourteen stab wounds had drained her life.

In the next room her fellow technician Patricia Matix lay dead from the same kind of wounds. Her husband accused me of not protecting his wife (He turned out to be the murderer.)

I had promised to "take care of the caregivers." Two lay dead. There was no avoiding the heartbreak we all felt at the violence that occurred amid a place dedicated to curing.

Abnormality is normal in hospitals. It takes a strong soul to invade a woman's body to deliver her newborn and later to be the one that may cut from that woman the ovaries that enabled conception.

Heart surgeons splay open chests to replace blocked arteries. To oncology nurses, cleaning chemotherapy-caused vomit may look as ugly as the cancer.

The brutality in caregiving begs for Beauty's hand.

But, "You have to be tough," many caregivers instruct. They are right unless "tough" means building a hard shell that blocks the beauty our souls need.

The most frequent gift visitors bring to patients is flowers. You need them too.

1

Principles of Radical Loving Care (RLC)

Definitions

RLC DEFINED: Radical Loving Care is the practice of The Golden Rule in a health care setting.

SERVANT'S HEART: Caregiving is a sacred calling practiced by those with a servant's heart.

SACRED ENCOUNTER: RLC is present when caregivers meet need with Love rather than indifference.

LOVE: We are all called to be children of Love, not victims of fear. Underlying all RLC is this: Live Love not fear.

GOLDEN THREAD: The healing thread of RLC flows through every loving caregiver—from the very first to all those living in the present and continues to those who are yet to come. This healing comes not *from* the caregiver but *through* them, and is evidence of Love's golden light.

HEALING HOSPITAL™: When caregivers in every department of a hospital embrace RLC, the focus of workplace culture shifts from illness and cure to Healing.

CULTURE IMPACT: The biggest determinant of caregiver behavior is work place culture.

LEADER'S ROLE: The first responsibility of a leader is to take care of the people who take care of people. Leaders bear the responsibility for creating a positive work place culture where RLC can take place.

THE MOTHER TEST™: The test of a Leader's success: Does *every* patient receive from *every* caregiver the kind of care we want for our mothers?

CULTURE CREATION: Passing The Mother Test requires establishing work place cultures that consistently reinforce loving care.

STORYTELLING: Stories signal values. The biggest indicator of loving culture is seen in the stories that are told.

RLC BALANCE: RLC puts compassion in balance with competence to create healing experiences. It shines through stories like The Good Samaritan.

POSITIVE LANGUAGE: Focus on what you love, not what you fear.

RENEWAL: The practice of Radical Loving Care requires constant refreshment & renewal and is nurtured by ritual.

The Foundation—Radical Loving Care

"How many leave hospitals healed of their physical illness but hurt in their feelings by the impersonal treatment they received?"

Henry Nouwen

I n these few words, Nouwen describes the need for Radical Loving Care and the Healing Hospital. In a Healing Hospital, Radical Loving Care transforms the focus from illness and cure to that of healing. RLC is the universal concept of Love applied in a health care setting.

For decades, hospitals have done an excellent job treating illness and injury. All too frequently, they have done a poor job of providing compassionate care. Radical Loving Care provides an approach to transforming health care from an assembly-line process to a series of meaningful meetings, of sacred encounters that bring a sense of healing to the vulnerable.

What do I mean by Love? It is a *universal* concept, not owned by any religion. It describes Beauty's energy in this world. The Buddha advised that, "The motivation of all religious practice is similar: love…" The apostle John wrote, "God is Love."(1 John 4:8)

If God is Love, how can you as a worldly being ever express it? Your human condition, with its endless appetites, consistently challenges Love's passage through you.

Fortunately, Radical Loving Care doesn't expect perfection. It recognizes the rich and difficult shadows in life as well as the light.

Because you exist by nature at the center of your own consciousness it takes work to recognize how you are balancing your needs with the needs of your fellow beings.

When you are fearful, your needs dominate your ability to live Love. At your best, you transcend your needs to relieve the suffering of another.

This is the challenge of Love. There is nothing more important.

The brilliant Rainer Maria Rilke wrote that "For one human being to love another: that is perhaps the most difficult task of all...*the work for which all other work is but preparation.*" (Emphasis mine)

Poets, apostles and saints are the ones you can look to for inspiration. But how can you as a so-called "ordinary" caregiver ever expect to express such a beautiful love?

Deep within you, with all your blessings and difficulties, lies the chance for you to clear your path so that Love, at least on occasion, can make its way through you.

My favorite American poet, Emily Dickinson, offered a shattering commentary in quiet words:

"The Love a life can show below
Is but a filament, I know,
Of that diviner thing
That faints upon the face of noon..."

You may engage that "filament," that Golden Thread, as you make your daily and nightly journey. As every traveler knows, the journey can be exhausting. You can only continue successfully if you pause, like a desert traveler, at the occasional oasis.

You are already on this journey.

Martin Luther King said that when you live Love you speak "The unarmed truth." Truth is its own protection.

Remember that Radical Loving Care is *God's Love expressed in the caregiving world.* It means living Love, not fear. It is radical because it is exceptional and therefore rare. Only the finest caregivers can sustain it.

Recall Rilke: "For one human being to love another: that is perhaps the most difficult task of all." That is why your travels are both more challenging and also more rewarding than anything else.

The biggest distinction between you and the machines you use to give care is Love. Computers can now program robots to do, or potentially do, almost everything a human can do except for one thing: to Love.

Doesn't this tell you that your life improves if you *increase your focus* on developing compassion to *balance* any obsessive focus on task performance? Doesn't this tell you that you can be a powerful expression of Love?

Do You Love Me?

Imagine how much more beautiful your life could be. Imagine living Love every day.

The earliest spring flowers are pioneers. Each April, they are the first to expose their vulnerable blossoms.

Sometimes, new forsythia are seared by a winter not ready to retreat. This may burn them but it never daunts them. Love is the gold we seek—enduring love. The pioneers among us take the highest risks to find it. When they succeed they are rewarded with life's richest gift. But, in the risking, they are always subject, like the forsythia, to pain.

We all want to love and be loved. We all hope to create life's finest union.

When two souls unite—whether for a few moments in a caregiving encounter or in a longer sacred relationship, can their love withstand winter's certain assault? Only when lovers survive storms can they know that God has crowned their union.

"...do you love me?" the resurrected Christ asked Peter (John 21:15-17) When Peter replied that he did, Jesus said, simply, "Feed my sheep."

Then Jesus asked him a second time and again a third. Each time Peter, with increasing irritation, protested that of course he loved Jesus.

Why did Christ persist? Of course, Peter had denied him three times *before* Jesus' death on the cross.

Why did Jesus tell Peter, "Feed my sheep"?

Herein lies your injunction. If you love God, you will Love those in need as well as those you desire.

This is the essence of a sacred encounter. When you help with holy intention you bless yourself and the other. Sympathy means to suffer another's pain. Only Love can empower survival.

If you think you love another ask yourself how you feel when trouble comes. If your love fades was it ever love?

There is no harder experience for caregivers than to love patients that spit at them, co-workers who betray them, and supervisors who punish instead of affirm.

Perhaps, this is why Love seems to be in hiding when, in the middle of spring, a beautiful bloom is suddenly struck by snow. Look again, the blossom is unbowed.

Liminal States

Why is the practice of Radical Loving Care so important for caregivers? A patient utters a simple four-word statement: "I am in pain." But, suffering is never simple.

Do you remember your worst pain? Do you recall how hard it was for you to experience that pain and to know that nobody else, in that moment, could understand?

This is the agony that isolation can produce. When your life struggles from breath to breath you may even believe it is not worth living. Why breathe again if such profound discomfort is to continue?

Pain is complex because illness casts you into a liminal state—an earthly purgatory. When you are ill you are, by definition, not well but you are also not dead. You are caught on the bridge between. Like a pilgrim, you lack the comfort of your homeland and you have not yet arrived in the new world.

The thunder of liminal states can feel unbearable. They create a particular desperation, a desire to be in one place or the other but not in between. It is an indescribable fear whose only antidote comes when Love arrives.

In this state of illness you remember the safe harbor of your homeland. You want the new land of healing to be better. Meanwhile you are caught, perhaps drowning, in the roiling ocean.

Who will help you? Your only lifeline is the caregiver. Your eyes beseech.

What will that caregiver bring to your burning soul?

This is the reason we invite you to sail into the waters of Radical Loving Care. The suffering need more than medicine. They need what only Love can provide—healing.

Cutting Yourself a Break—The Reality of Fatigue, Irritability & Hostility

Love is such an intense experience that I often worry that books and speeches about love and caring set up an ideal that feels impossible. You're already working hard. Why pursue an ideal thought unachievable?

Fortunately for you, you don't need to be a saint. Indeed, the saints often fell victim to the same kinds of fatigue, irritability and anger that afflict you and me.

The concept of Radical Loving Care doesn't call you to be perfect, or even to try to be perfect. In fact, "trying" as a way of succeeding, can be a trap.

For example, you know that when you try not to be angry, this may actually cause you to build up resentment. I can tell you from my own frequent lapses that the same is true with irritability and other obnoxious behaviors.

The best coping skill with a rude patient is not to say to oneself, "This guy is a jerk but I have to be better than he is and be polite."

Instead, Love suggests rethinking what's underneath another person's anger and how that is never about us. The often hard-to-find key is to *let Love* inform your behavior.

Yielding to Love's energy is the only way to deal successfully with your fear and resentment. This kind of letting go of ego calls you to step out of the way, to become a sort of observer as Love strengthens your heart.

As I've indicated, I'm not any better at living Love than are you (and may well be worse.) This book is not about telling you anything new. You already know as much (or more) about Love as I do.

What *do* you want to know? How do you want to change? Do you even *want* to alter the course of your life?

These are the questions we are here to explore together. The answers that matter will not come from me but from you.

The hope of this writing is to help you live the kind of Love you want to express in your life.

Stay with this work.

Love is the best your life has to offer.

2

Golden Rule Care & "Gold Rules" Care

"Often it is the ordinary…in life's experience that combines with an unusually sensitive temperament…to produce a heightened sense of awareness."

Kay Redfield Jamison, Ph.D.

Recently, I watched a replay of one of our age-old human struggles in microcosm—an "ordinary life experience" if ever there was one. My two-year-old grandson had something his five-year-old sister wanted. She asked for it, he declined.

Look at *some* of her choices in this ordinary situation: 1) She could grab it, 2) She could ask a parent to intervene, 3) She could negotiate, 4) She could divert him and swipe it, 5) She could wait until he was tired of it and move in, or 6) She could decide his happiness was important, let him keep it, and help him enjoy it.

Nearly three, he is just old enough to know that he has the same set of choices in reverse. As a little brother, I, too, learned the younger one has his own kind of leverage.

How many times have you been in this type of situation across your life? How many times today will you engage in these kinds of transactions with adults?

Is this childhood conflict different from the drama played out among world leaders every day? When Palestine and Israel or the United States and North Korea disagree, how do their kinds of options differ from the ones available to my grandchildren?

Perhaps the contrast is only one of scale.

It's remarkable how early we learn to view the world as a set of transactions. "I will do this for you if (and only if) you do this for me."

If I do something for you, I expect you to thank me. If you don't, I may be angry and decide to dislike you.

This type of transactional thinking pervades our lives. Every adult knows the Golden Rule: "Do unto others as you would have them do unto you." Unfortunately, we've also all heard the trite takeoff on it: "He who has the gold make the rules."

Love teaches us to give. The world teaches us to take.

Not everyone "gets" the idea of Radical Loving Care, but everyone knows the Golden Rule.

Radical Loving Care is Golden Rule Care.

Your life struggle pits your human appetite against Love's energy. If you are going to let go of your own needs in order to help another, you want something in return—perhaps a paycheck, but at least a thank you.

Most hospital leaders (the ones perceived as having all the gold and making all the rules) want everyone on their staff to give loving care. Most caregivers would like that too. Both groups want something in return. Leaders want successful performance. Caregivers want (at least) to be paid for their hard work.

In addition, caregivers want something that doesn't cost a troy ounce of gold: They want to be appreciated. It's remarkable how few leaders understand this.

We would all want everyone to live Love. Reality tells us this is too much to expect from human beings whose needs often push the other way.

So how do we motivate caregivers to live the hard teaching of the Golden Rule?

At a conceptual level, you can imagine why living Love is better than existing in fear. At a practical level, you think in transactions: If I don't act right, I may be fired. If I do act right, I expect something in return.

The two biggest things leaders can do to grow Love's energy are: 1) Create cultures where loving care is common and expected, and 2) Show caregivers why living Love is in their best interest.

> *The two biggest things leaders can do to grow Love's energy are: 1) Create cultures where loving care is common and expected, and 2) Show caregivers why living love is in their best interest.*

Here's your reason to live Love—In the long run, you feel better when you give Love rather than when you take from someone else.

It sounds like something we might preach to our children. What if we tried it ourselves?

Of course, this is an example where knowing the rule and honoring it do not make it easier to practice it. That's the reason you need to focus your energy on the practice of Love.

The Silver Rule

Love is a natural force. Much of your human condition blocks Love's practice because your body is always telling you what YOU want, not what someone else might need from you.

There's only one exception to the obvious—it's that not everyone wants care of exactly the same kind we want.

This is **The Silver Rule**: Be sensitive to what kind of care your patient wants from you. Their wants may not be the same as yours.

Organizing Love

Radical Loving Care calls us to organize Love so that Love's expression is structured and disciplined in such a way as to be effective.

Nature organizes the expression of Beauty into a flower. The flower is not Beauty. It is an *expression* of Beauty.

The care given by the Good Samaritan is not Love. It is an expression of Love.

The decision you make today to let Love flow through you into a person in need is not Love itself. It is *your choice* to let go of your agenda so that Love may make its transit through you and into another.

This matters because it tells you that Love is like the elements of the earth. The air is free flowing until you sew a sail to catch it—to allow it—to move your boat across the lake.

Water moves mindless of our needs. We shape cups to drink it. Beyond that, if we attend to the design of the cup we may catch Beauty in it as well as water.

The earth lies ready but will not feed us until we pick or plant or mix. The earth will shelter us and support our endeavors if we structure buildings to sit on it.

Across three decades of leading hospitals, it came clear to me that how we organize our expressions of Love (our culture) affects Love's power in this world.

A hospital, hospice or nursing home can organize itself to deliver services. But Love will find no traction there unless leaders support the hiring of employees with a Servant's Heart and the training of caregivers on how to live loving care. Neither can Love find its way through caregivers' hands and into patients' hearts unless the healthcare *culture* is structured to support Love's energy.

The crucial application of this idea comes when you consider structuring Love's expression through yourself. If my thoughts are patterned to determine what I will get for myself out of each encounter, *Love will not appear* because the intention underneath transactions is personal gain, not loving service.

Healing healthcare organizations grow in a structure organized by loving leaders. The goal is to plant the seeds of loving caregiving and nourish them to bloom in a setting where healing, beyond curing, may thrive.

The Transcendent Caregiver

*"If human beings had no capacity for **self-transcendence**, they would be mere fields of instinctual experience…contributing nothing by way of initiative or creativity to their ongoing life."* (Emphasis mine)

Edward Farley

Who are the caregivers you want to come to you in times of your deepest suffering and highest joy? How are they created and nurtured?

According to Farley each of us has the capacity for self-transcendence. In order to heal the suffering of others we need to accomplish this transcendence by placing the needs of others above our own.

Yet, the same world that lifted your body into life simultaneously weighs on you, forever challenging your ability to go beyond your own needs to meet those of another.

Only a small number among us can consistently place the needs of others first. They are the true heroes of caregiving. They are the ones who live lives of Radical Loving Care.

Why Change? The Path to Light—Our Most Sacred Journey

"I close my eyes in order to see."

Paul Gauguin

Because of her nightly rounds to check on the wounded during the Crimean War, the most famous image of Florence Nightingale casts her as "The Lady with the Lamp." The image is powerful for caregivers not only because Nightingale founded modern nursing, but also because we know that the lamp symbolizes the search we all pursue to find "The Light." The Light Nightingale sought was a system that would bring healing to all those in need.

Nightingale was an explorer. The journeys of the world's saints and pioneers offer fascinating stories and are wonderful metaphors that can inform for each of us our personal search.

Explorer Ponce de Leon spent his career searching Florida (which he named) for the Fountain of Youth. Columbus, of course, sought a new route to India. In both cases, the explorers found something *different* and more important than what they sought. Neither recognized the value of their discoveries.

Perhaps most famous of all searches in the Western world has centered on the pursuit of the mystical cup that, according to legend, Jesus used at the Last Supper and Joseph of Arimathea later used to catch the blood of Jesus. This is the Holy Grail of legend—a thing so precious that many lives have been lost seeking it.

Each story is of a quest.

You have to make your way through the traffic of patients each day. Why bother with such stories?

When you look at your own story, don't you want it to include your own pathway to "The Light?"

Frustrated, tired of trying, or perhaps believing there is no such path, you may sometimes feel like giving up. But, if you are reading this, you are continuing your travels.

Good. There is no more important journey than your own one towards The Light. If you give up, you fall into the half-light of a world devoid of real meaning.

The single most important thing to know is that The Light is always there, waiting for you to find her. You must rediscover your path to her every day.

What does "The Light" look like to you? Is it peace and serenity? Does it lie in the eyes of a healed patient? Does it live in a glimpse of the sea? Does it flow from the music of a laugh or through the paint on an artist's canvas? Does it circle your heart when you are in the presence of the one you love?

All of these experiences tell you that although The Light may be awakened from without, it lives within.

As the artist Paul Gauguin wrote, you must close your eyes in order to see it.

The Risk of Spiritual Atrophy

"But we who would be born again indeed, must wake our souls unnumbered times a day."

George MacDonald

Why else is your journey important? Caregivers may search for The Light more than others do simply because caregiving's endless demands hold a hidden risk. **Protocols can be monotonous. Soon, Spiritual Atrophy may settle in. Color can fade into a gray life.**

"Here comes another body," I heard a recovery nurse say one morning as I did my rounds through her area. Indeed, that's what the unconscious patient looked like. Deprived of everyday reality by anesthetics, the patient appeared comatose.

I watched this nurse perform her tasks as matter-of-factly as if she were cooking a hamburger. Her eyes were dead as a subway rider. Her tone was flat. Since I have never been a first line caregiver, I can only sympathize with her challenges.

"How long have you been a recovery nurse?" I asked.

"Twenty years," she responded with a sense of fatigue rather than energy.

"Have you ever thought about working in another area?"

"Not anymore," she answered. "I'm pretty much stuck here."

At the age of forty-three, she appeared to be "stuck" in that area for another twenty-two years. She may be one that counts the minutes until her shift ended, the days until the weekend, the months until retirement.

It's easy to see why anyone for whom work has become a chore might be tired. Amid daily fatigue, generating the energy to reignite your soul with new approaches may seem both too hard and too complicated.

My heart breaks for the millions of caregivers who have fallen into this trap. What may have been an exciting challenge in its dawning has become Chinese Water Torture.

Equally tragic are caregivers who live in fear. Their daily lives feel threatened by anxiety over the risk of mistakes and over worry that the boss will punish them or, worse, fire them. Crossfire from fellow caregivers may also drain hope.

Even at young ages, change can be difficult. Life grabs hold of us rapidly teaching its basic lessons: seek pleasure, avoid pain, cultivate comfort, be happy, and "don't rock the boat!"

The older we become, the longer we have been in the same job, the more challenging change becomes. For those who have chosen careers in caregiving, Spiritual Atrophy may begin as early as five years into the work.

Caregiving roles teach protocols. Protocols swiftly become routines. Routines can define boredom.

"Christ! What are patterns for?" Amy Lowell wrote in a poem that touches on killing in World War I.

Daily patterns may be helpful but they may also dilute your soul's strength. Patterned thinking can become the enemy of the kind of fresh living that keeps compassion alive. Rote behavior can lead you to do some jobs with less than ten percent of your attention.

In his book *Man's Search for Meaning* Victor Frankl quotes Friedrich Nietzsche's "He who has a why can bear almost any how." It is your "why" that gives you the will to live against life's most crushing setbacks.

That is the reason to change. If you are "dying" in your work and in your everyday life you need to find a new "why."

How do you become a care *lover* rather than a care hater?

Compassion Fatigue & New Energy

The answer at the core of caregiver's woes comes from Dr. Frankl. He details how the concentration camp victims who survived the best were fueled by a belief that their life had meaning. Attached to that meaning was an enduring hope.

Death came rapidly to those who uttered the three-word phrase, "I give up."

In the same recovery room with the spiritually flat-lined nurse was another veteran caregiver whose joy was striking. I noticed immediately that she was speaking to her unconscious patient as she turned him, adjusted his tubes and stroked his face. Of course, this patient would remember nothing of this nurse's compassionate behavior. But, speaking to him was a constant signal to her that she was caring for a human being, not a "body."

"How do you keep up your energy in this job?" I asked.

"It's not a job," she answered. "This is my calling."

For the tired nurse, it's just a job. For the tired nurse, the patient before her is "just a body." For the tired nurse, every task is a routine.

So long as the nurse sees her patient as a body, she will see her work as someone who "cares for bodies."

Can the tired nurse change? Yes, if she or he is supported by a culture of caring in which compassion fatigue is understood...

For the energized nurse, her work is a calling. For the energized nurse, the patient before her is a human being in an altered state. For the energized nurse, every action is done to give the patient the best experience possible in that moment.

As long as the energized nurse sees her patient as a *person* in an altered state, she will define her calling as caring for sick people who need her help.

Love brings enormous results. Fear paralyzes our days.

Can the tired nurse change? The answer is yes, if she or he is supported by a culture of caring—one where the risk of compassion fatigue is understood by leadership and one where leaders and caregivers are trained to understand *new ways of seeing old work*.

This is the work of Radical Loving Care—to develop cultures where caregiving is an honor, not a chore; to awaken everyone in that culture to new ways of seeing people in patient gowns, to support caregivers in understanding that all of their work is sacred.

Radical Loving Care brings a new dawn into the lives of harried caregivers. It brings renewed meaning. It brings hope.

3

Pointing To a Path for Leaders

"...the trouble with most inspirational books is that you can feel them trying to inspire you..."

Anatole Broyard in *Intoxicated by My Illness*

I nspiring without changing behavior is a risk that haunts *Radical Loving Care*. Will this work truly rearrange the tectonic plates of your heart in the way that radical love requires?

The new medical-industrial complex makes change more and more difficult. Still, inspired leadership can lead change if they start from the right place and engage in a sustained effort.

Inside Radical Loving Care seeks to distill Love's concepts into one principle...

The best this writing can do for you is to point you to your own discovery. Psychoanalytic constructs are of limited value in creating culture change. You need to find *your* path to this different and challenging way of being in the world.

Nearly four centuries ago Thomas Traherne wrote, **"God is present by Love alone."** The story of the Good Samaritan can teach everyone—not just people who call themselves Christians. The story traces the path we all need to follow, the path that is informed by defining love as helping others *beyond* expectations. Read the parable carefully and you will see the heart that drives the extra effort that is Love's highest expression.

Recognizing your demands means that *Inside Radical Loving Care* is a handbook to help you live Love's concepts abiding by **one principle**, Radical Loving Care, and a set of ideas and actions that can be practical guides for you in creating a healing environment for yourself and others. That is the reason for highlighting what has turned out to be the most transformative concept for success: **"The Mother Test."**

It does not require an earthquake to shift healthcare cultures. Instead, a laser focus on concepts and strategies can bring change *across years*—change that will transform your life and the health of the patients who come to you in need.

Transformation will not occur simply because leaders announce it. Organizations need to grow new **Radical Loving Care (RLC) Teams** to ignite and spread the power of loving care.

Although change comes person by person, there are often thousands of people in a given healthcare organization. Change needs to be leveraged and supported.

The Cultural Tipping Point—The Four Choices

The moment where momentum starts to move toward a culture dominated by loving care is the well-known "Tipping Point" first described by author Malcolm Gladwell. You may not actually notice the actual tipping point when it arrives.

Yet, at some moment, you will observe that things are changing for the better. That means it's time to pour it on fueled by the optimism that you have gained traction.

The core decision for you is to assess where you are right now and to determine if that is where you want to be. Are you able to pass The Mother Test? Are you living Golden Rule Care?

You must decide how committed you are to meaningful change. If you aren't, there is no point in reading further. If you are, there is a powerful pathway you can follow.

The encouraging news is that you don't need one hundred percent support to move a group. The number is more like forty or fifty percent. If you can lead up to half your group into the new cultural mindset and action set of Radical Loving Care, the rest of the group (except about ten to fifteen percent who are hard core negative) will come along.

Understanding How to Transform Culture

The first choice is to become **aware** that the current culture of your team or your life is not what you want it to be. Along with this is to decide if you believe in the idea of Radical Loving Care (or Meaning Care or Golden Rule Care or whatever else you decide to call it.)

The second choice is to **accept** the truth that it is possible for you to change yourself, your team or your organizational culture so that patient care improves.

The third choice is to **imagine** what your new self, team or culture would look like if Radical Loving Care were integrated into your life. What would change? How do you like the look of the new picture? Do you want to become a Healing Hospital instead of a place where the focus is merely on "fixing" patient's problems?

The fourth choice is the **action** stage. It's time to put this new vision into action.

Engineering Change through "The Intensives"

Because the Radical Loving Care approach marks a significant difference in the way you do things, success can only come for you by starting with a series of "Intensives." These are a series of sessions (with teams and organizational leaders) in which you perform a deep study of the first three steps above.

Each session also tracks the four choices. Each stage will require regular revisits.

Initial Audit and Criteria

Start by establishing criteria for yourself and your RLC teams. As teams regularly pass The Mother Test, organization-wide culture begins to move. If teams aren't succeeding, leaders need to ask why and to help support each group in reaching the new, Radical Loving Care standard.

A baseline is critical. This means each team must be evaluated and rated. Each leader and each individual must be reviewed to determine if they are living a Servant's Heart.

You also need to look within and review the four choices at a personal level. How are you doing meeting the criteria you want to establish for others?

Meanwhile, in order for an organization to pass The Mother Test, signal that *a **new** standard has been established.* With full recognition of the fine work done in the past, the organization needs to be clear about this new standard so that each caregiver understands what is expected in the new era.

Here's the central path I point you to: *Live Love, not fear.* Live The Mother Test, and every other idea about the practice of Radical Loving will emerge. Create a culture that graces the people who come to you in need.

Change Requirements

Culture changes when that which shapes culture is first determined, and then changed. For leaders, culture is determined by elements like:

1) Leadership Tone and Focus, 2) Hiring, 3) Training, 4) Annual or quarterly employee reviews, 5) Leadership Rounding, 6) Storytelling, 7) The Language of Leadership and talk among first line staff, 8) The decisions made to

celebrate the best and either change or eliminate the worst, and 8) Examining the Content of Meeting Agendas.

There are a dozen other factors that develop as the process moves forward.

Are you leading and hiring with a servant's heart? Can your team pass The Mother Test? Is there someone you *want* caring for your mother? Is there a caregiver you do *not* want caring for your mother? If so, why are they on staff? How would hiring change if this element were intensified?

Most important, what if you reorganized your team to 1) **celebrate the successful**, 2) give the middle group a chance to improve, and 3) **remove those you do not want caring for you mother?**

Do these things and the culture *will* change.

Your organization will perform much better. This means you will move toward accomplishing the most important goal you have—improving patient care.

Our Most Sacred Place

The most sacred place within you is also the most secret. It is the hidden chamber of your pain. Your scars are stirred when you encounter the agony of another.

Many run from this darkness. Caregivers cannot.

Caregivers need to enter the other's darkness in order to help the wounded find healing. There is a hidden reward for this. It comes in the joy that floods their hearts when they are able to relieve another's suffering.

It is up to you to decide whether or not to open your heart to this greatest of all powers. The door to this gift is covered with so many warnings that most leave it shut. It requires courage to open it and to keep it open because of the struggle healers undergo to understand that healing comes from within.

Medical training teaches the opposite. It teaches that once you have skill you can cure and your job is done. You practice your skill. Presto, some people are *cured.* The most sensitive caregivers quickly discover that skill can heal injured skin but not a wounded heart.

Only a loving heart can heal a scarred one.

To create art your heart needs to hold the hand of skill. To heal requires an artist's passion.

The power to create, to love, and to heal lives in you. It awaits awakening.

Competence enters through one door. Compassion enters the same room through another. When the two are married in a sacred encounter, Radical Loving Care is born.

To mend damaged hearts, surgeons have to force their way into our bodies using both saws and scalpels. They cut to cure.

Compassion's energy will not appear through force or command. It waits to be invited and will only enter a heart that is open.

Let Love open your heart.

A Word about the "Love" Word

Gender differences often impact the use of the "love" word. In my long experience, the complaints I've heard about the use of this word always come from men.

Remember: The core concept of Radical Loving Care can be stated in one, four-word sentence: **Live Love, not fear.** How many of your daily decisions are grounded in fear?

My heart bleeds for any caregiver who comes to work everyday fearing a supervisor or a chronically angry physician. What does it mean to have a staff that not only practices love but, actually uses the word?

"I'm not going to use the 'love' word," a male physician told me after I introduced Radical Loving Care at a physician seminar. Of course, it's better to live love and not use the word than it is to use the word and not live it. But why not do both?

Some of my fellow males have even wondered if the love word is inappropriate because it might suggest something sexual (as if genuine caregiving could possibly have such an implication.) Others are simply uneasy. One physician leader at the Cleveland Clinic even said to me, "Can't we just call it compassion? Do we have to call it love?"

The answer is yes. This is caregiving, not football or warfare.

At the same time we don't want to cheapen the word, to drain it of meaning by overuse (as in the case of the once elegant word "awesome" whose chronic use has ruined its power.)

The reason leaders and caregivers need to use the Love word is partly because of its very rarity amid the techno-lingo in our medical industrial complex.

The second reason leaders need to encourage the use of the word Love is that its utterance signals the earthquake shift needed to move cultures. Once spoken, however, Love's definition needs to be lived or it will become meaningless and a cause for cynicism.

Love means *competence* as well as *compassion*. Love should never be limited to soft gestures.

Instead, it should be thought of in the love language of Dr. Martin Luther King, Jr. who said, **"We must always be both tough-minded and tender-hearted."**

There is no energy that is more powerful and important than love. Why shouldn't we engage this energy, and the word that encompasses it in the crucial work of caring for the sick and wounded?

Communities of Caring

> *When your organization shows that its top value is loving care then it becomes a true community of caring.*

Hospitals, hospices and nursing homes are like villages. The typical services of a village, healthcare, security, restaurants, and housekeeping, live in these organizations in addition to high-level specialty services. Like cities, they are open twenty-four hours a day every day of the year.

Health care settings can operate like factories making widgets or like ideal villages where people care for each other in the common goal of creating a caring community. In any case, *patients have a right to expect more than a safe visit and the latest technology.*

Health care organizations can create communities of caring more easily than can towns because they can decide who gets to become (and remain) a "citizen." Every community has a culture. When your organization shows that its top value is loving care, then it becomes a true community of caring.

The Shift

What causes you to shift in ways that open you to healing or to bursts of creativity? You know that some process is required.

Mother Theresa relied on prayer. In this state, she reports moments of reverie that brought her into the kind of dreamlike state that allowed her to meet God.

She also knew that her searing encounters with the poorest of the poor could crack open a pathway for Love to travel through her and into the hearts of lepers, the dying, and the starving children haunting the back alleys of Calcutta.

Artists often use strange tricks to kick-start their creativity. Charles Dickens, author of countless classics, including *A Christmas Carol*, thinking that magnetic forces helped him to create, turned his bed to the north.

Beethoven poured cold water over his head, believing it stimulated his brain.

Whatever their method of achieving it, all artists understand that it is reverie that can open them to Beauty's energy where they can discover and begin to incubate the ideas that will touch our souls.

> *When a personal shift towards Love occurs it must be reinforced by ritual every day.*

The sages among us engage reverie in their journey to healing and to Beauty. Inside this reverie they can *imagine what Love looks like* and translate it into this world for us to appreciate or ignore.

You can celebrate the healers and the artists. And you can learn from them how you may, each short day and long night, find your way into the light.

4

Concepts & Rules
in Cultural Transformation

We say common sense must be our guide. Yet such sense is too often uncommon and even less often lived out in practice.

> **Remember:**
> **The biggest distinction between humans and machines is Love.**

In 1976 when I was serving as legal counsel for an inner city hospital as well as a Vice President, I received an odd call one winter night.

The doctor who called from the Emergency Room was relatively new to the United States and very anxious to follow the rules: "Mr. Chapman," she said frantically, "I have a patient who is hemorrhaging. Can I go ahead and treat her?"

"What are you asking?" I inquired.

"She's unconscious and can't give consent."

Of course, I told her to hang up the phone and treat the patient immediately. Life threatening emergencies generally forestall the need for consent. Rules can confuse the best-intentioned caregivers.

History is replete with examples where rule-breaking was required to bring important change. The Indian Freedom movement led by Gandhi in the first half of the twentieth century, the Civil Rights movement in the United States in the 1950s and '60s, and the fight against Apartheid in South Africa during the 1970s are just a few examples.

Of course, in order to follow God's law, Jesus himself broke countless rules.

How do we know when to "break" the rules?

Loving care must guide every decision. Below are concepts that provide help to caregivers who are seeking the best for those who are suffering. Ultimately, the true caregivers are willing to take the consequences for breaking a rule to help a patient as well as for following one when it is in the patient's best interests.

Core Concepts

It's not clear that listing things to do can generate something as amorphous as loving behavior. Still, caregivers are trained using principles and rules and some are helpful in growing cultures of loving care.

The Golden Thread

The Golden Thread is the tradition of healing that began when the first caregiver reached out to meet the needs of another rather than his or her own. It ran through the hands of the first caregivers and now travels through ours. We can honor this thread and its precious grace or we can break it.

Each of us can either run with the baton handed us by the ancestors of loving care or we can drop the baton and quit, and plodding along with the baton is the same as dropping it.

Although Love is an eternal energy, its expression in the world requires that it flow through your earthbound self. Like a garden, it requires constant tending. Every gardener knows that there is never a moment when the plants can be ignored, when he or she can say, "I have nurtured the garden to Beauty and now my work is done."

Radical Loving Care is the gift given by every person who walks in the footprints of the Good Samaritan. It lives in the courage of the caregiver who travels the rocky ground and then reaches into the blood of fear to try and heal a wounded heart.

The Golden Thread sews together the fabric of high quality caregiving.

The Golden Thread sews together the fabric of high quality caregiving.

Caregivers engage in some of the most intimate kinds of touching we can imagine. They reach through the private openings into our bodies. They regularly brave the sights and smells of blood and tissue and bone to deliver babies and comfort the dying. They hold cancer-ridden bodies, run catheters into our bladders and reach into our chests to fix our damaged hearts.

They also clean up the products of caring for illness and injury.

At Riverside Methodist Hospital I had the honor one day of supporting our nursing staff in delivering a baby. This experience, of course, is one to be celebrated and honored.

Afterwards, I was reveling in the glow of my chance to see a newborn enter the world when a housekeeper holding a mop approached me with a sly grin.

"Do you want to come help me clean up now?" she asked. I turned away from the room that must have held blood and afterbirth.

Everyone is a caregiver. Everyone holds The Golden Thread.

The Sacred Encounter

Imagine two circles. The caregiver occupies one. The other holds the person in need.

Overlap the circles. A Sacred Encounter occurs every time love embraces need.

If the caregiver brings nothing but cold competence, the encounter is simply a transaction. If the caregiver brings love, the encounter becomes sacred.

There is no need to dramatize the use of a word as powerful as sacred. In many ways, it is important to demystify this crucial idea.

If "sacred" is thought of only in a religious context it becomes too easy for cynics to disregard it. If the word sacred is off-putting for you try words like spiritual, meaningful or even "light-filled."

Rethink the quality of your relationships. Caregivers have enormous power. Physically, they are upright before patients who are lying or sitting below them. They hold curative knowledge versus a patient who may know little. They are healthy. The patient is not.

Caregivers can be like prison guards or they can be healers.

Too often, caregivers squander their power. In fact, their very arrival before a suffering soul carries the potential for the immediate onset of healing.

Amid one childhood illness (it was in the days of house calls), I lay suffering in my bed awaiting the doctor's arrival. The moment he crossed the threshold into my room, I noticed that I was feeling better. His very presence brought healing energy.

The same is true of any caregiver (including housekeeper, x-ray techs, financial staff and electricians.) The moment we enter the room of an ill person or encounter a team member we bring our energy. When a nurse enters the room with a glum, impatient, over-efficiency her or his energy will pull down the patient's.

Hospitals, hospices and nursing homes are frightening to patients. Why not add *compassion* to your *competence?*

Length of time does not govern whether an encounter is sacred. One can happen in the touch of a caring hand, in a moment of eye contact or with the use of a few kind words.

> *A Sacred Encounter occurs every time love embraces need.*

Transforming ER Encounters—An Example

A person enters a hospital emergency room writhing in pain. Holding her side she limps up to the admitting clerk.

What do you think most clerks would say? Sadly, most people guess that the first words would be, "Name? Insurance card?" and then "Take a seat. We will call you when we are ready."

I've asked admitting clerks about these transactions. Naturally, these are typically kind people who would never want to offend a suffering soul.

The system has beaten them down.

"I used to be friendly to patients like that," one clerk told me. "But, a supervisor told me I was taking too much time."

How much time does it take to give loving care? What if the admitting clerk began like this: "I'm so sorry to see you are in pain. We'll get this bit of paper work over quickly and take care of you as fast as we can."

These are the kind of words that can lift transactions into loving care. Supervisors trained in this kind of thinking establish cultures where caregivers think of the right words on their own.

There is nothing more meaningful to both patients and caregivers than cultivating Sacred Encounters. It is in these meetings that caregiving goes beyond fixing and touches the hem of healing. It is here that a job becomes sacred work.

The Servant's Heart

The biggest way to change culture for the better is to hire for a servant's heart. In fact, this extends to every decision leadership can make to develop excellence.

Hire for a Servant's Heart, orient for one, train for one, reward each one. Consider the quality of the Servant's Heart in annual reviews, in promotions and demotions and in team performance.

Staff members who carry a Servant's Heart think about giving the right medications (versus the negative thinking that simply considers "avoiding" mistakes.) They are the ones we want caring for those we love.

Why hire anyone who doesn't have a Servant's Heart? Why keep them on your team?

The Servant's Heart knows about Love. With the right support, they will consistently deliver the best care.

> *Hire for a Servant's Heart, orient for one, train for one, reward each one.*

The Five Relationships

People who work in healing environments look at sacred encounters in the context of five key relationships.

1.Caregiver to Patient

This is the primary relationship. It is the basis for our entire system of care.

If sacred encounters don't happen here, the rest of the relationships don't matter. Note here that *if the basic attitude of the caregiver is grounded in Love then even transactional encounters take on tones of healing.*

2.Caregiver to Caregiver

Complex healthcare is delivered through teams. Healing healthcare organizations work consciously to nurture team development.

To pass The Mother Test team members need to support each other, to encourage each other, to fill in for exhausted colleagues, to express to patients what the patient is counting on: To know that they are in the hands of a great team of caregivers. In other words, the team needs to live Love, not fear.

3. Caregiver to Leader

The single most important responsibility of every healthcare leader is *to take care of the people who take care of people.* Every leader who truly succeeds practices this principle.

The principle is simple: Take great care of caregivers and they will give patients great care.

4. Caregiver to Environment

The caregiving environment usually presents enormous challenges. Florescent lighting, long, linoleum-clad hallways, beeping monitors, and difficult aromas attend illness settings.

Most caregivers are women. Most women work to warm up their environments and their male counterparts often follow suit. Family photos appear in the nursing station. So do childhood drawings, small stuffed animals and team logos.

Leaders have a much bigger responsibility. The best ones consult talented architects who understand how to design caregiving environments that support healing.

5. Caregiver to Self – The Importance of Compassion Fatigue

In many ways, this last-listed relationship should come first. Leaders need to take care of caregivers. *Caregivers need to take care of themselves.*

In a landmark study conducted several years back by the Drs. Glaser at Ohio State University demonstrated the stress caregivers are under. The study was divided into two groups.

Group A had no caregiving responsibilities. Group B was made up of people involved in direct caregiving.

A small wound was made on the arm of each participant. Wound recovery times were measured over the next several weeks.

On average, the arm wound on the caregivers in Group B took *nine times longer to heal* than did the wounds on the arms of those in Group A.

Compassion fatigue is a genuine risk. Caregivers who don't take care of themselves can lapse into job burnout, increased risks of mistakes, even an overall malaise that can lead to illness. Worn out caregivers cannot give patients the care they need nor can they bring their best to the other relationships crucial to good caregiving.

Many caregivers are terrible at this. They constantly short-change themselves on the grounds that the patient not only comes first but that they come in last.

Arriving home exhausted from a twelve-hour shift, many caregivers are immediately confronted with caregiving responsibilities at home. "I can't take time for myself," they tell me. "That would be selfish."

When my son was six weeks old I sat on plane with him in my lap. Before the plane took off, the flight attendant took the microphone and began the litany of rules so familiar most passengers tune them out.

I was doing the same until she said this: "If the plane loses altitude oxygen masks will drop down."

Leaping ahead to her next sentence, I immediately assumed I could guess her next words. She would, of course, tell us that if we were traveling with a small child we should put the mask on them first.

As you know, this is the wrong answer. The mask goes on the caregiver first. *If the caregiver isn't getting enough oxygen, how can she or he look after anyone else?*

Clear as this is, caregivers ignore it. If we truly absorbed the importance of self-care we would take every opportunity to engage rest, meditation, exercise, diet and healthy relationship – spiritually as well as with others.

Culture change only occurs when each and every caregiver nurtures love of self. In a religious context, this means accepting that we are all children of God. In a universal context, this means that we are at our best when we act as pathways for Love's transit.

> *Culture change only occurs when each and every caregiver nurtures love of self.*

Self-Care through Cultivating the Arts and Spiritual Life

A healthy spiritual life is essential to the delivery of loving care. Since we think of the heart as the source of compassion, this source needs nurturing from the spirit.

Religion is one pathway but certainly not the only one. Others may prefer an independent approach. In both cases loving caregivers know their life must be guided from within.

Since I personally believe that God is Love, I use Love in my thinking to represent God. That is why I capitalize the word and use it as a proxy for God's presence. The word Love may also have less baggage than the word "God."

The reason art appreciation helps caregiving is that the arts teach us to appreciate the world, in spite of its troubles, as a place of Love.

Art can only be appreciated through a respectful approach. Anyone who rushes past the viewing of a painting will miss a meaningful encounter with the artist.

Art cannot reach those in a hurry.

Art appreciation requires us to slow down. It teaches us how to connect listening, seeing, and every other sense to our souls.

Loving care and its practices, touch, listening, the use of the right words, the development of our highest skills— none of this can be understood on the run.

Spiritual practices help us stay in touch with the Love that lives within. Love can only come from Love.

Transforming Culture

Cultural transformation starts with a deep leadership commitment. The tough hierarchy of healthcare organizations demonstrates that trans-organizational change will not occur unless top leadership embraces loving care.

The overall principle gains quick acceptance. Every leader tells me there is no more important energy than Love.

Every CEO tells me that every patient should be treated with loving care that marries competence with compassion.

Few leaders deliver.

Part of the problem stems from the fact that, for most of us, our first caregiving encounter was with our mothers. It was from them that we received the nurturing that taught us what it means to put others ahead of self.

Perhaps that is why ninety-six percent of nurses are women. Women make up eighty percent of the staff of hospitals, hospices and nursing homes.

The problem is that men lead about eighty percent of health care organizations. It's not that men don't understand the concept of caregiving. It's that too often males focus on competition instead of caregiving.

One of the first things I heard from some of the men running a hospital I took over was that we had to "beat the other hospitals." We had to take their market share. We had to win higher patient satisfaction scores. We had to conquer. (One leader actually referred to one of our competitors as "the evil empire.")

Men need to be both "tough-minded and tender-hearted" to embrace the hard work of loving care. So do women. The work of transforming a culture is too difficult to engage in half measures.

Loving leaders focus on succeeding by improving the organization they are running, not by obsessively focusing on the competition. The three hospital systems I was privileged to lead developed extraordinary cultures of loving care and phenomenal success—clinically and financially as well as (or perhaps because of) world class patient and employee satisfaction.

Fortunately, leaders can be taught how to build healing hospitals.

First comes the need for every CEO in the country, male or female, to accept that Love belongs at the center. CEO's are not military generals committed to killing enemy soldiers and they are not football coaches dedicated to beating the opposing team.

There are a range of strategies and tactics required for change. The ones I describe are field-tested and have been successful in a wide variety of setting.

Everyone in an organization adapts an approach in their setting. Once leadership has set the right tone, it is up to every team to take on the challenge. The most important change happens (or not) inside the heart of each caregiver.

At the most practical level you may ask, what's in this for me? In the truest part of yourself you already know the answer.

Go through the motions and you are facing a career life empty of meaning. Express loving care in your work and your job becomes a calling.

5

The Transformative Power of Stories

"In the telling of their stories, strangers befriend not only their host but also their own past."

Henry Nouwen

Importance of Detail and Honesty

Stories told with rich detail and raw honesty hold the power to change your life. They signal your values. Those told in organizations do the same.

If your *only* stories speak of budgets, charts, and technology, then how can compassion thrive within you and around you?

Consider the impact of a story or a poem when it is not just *read,* but is *experienced* in the context of one of Liz Wessel's brilliant mandalas in the *Journal of Sacred Work.*

When you figure out what a story means to *you,* you own it. When you own it, you are likely to *live* the truth of the story.

Stories help you live Love, not fear. Since they report what you value, they signal the care you want for your mother.

Story I—Heartbreak & Triumph

"His mother didn't want him," the internationally renowned spoken word artist Minton Sparks told me one day. She was describing the early twentieth century story of a great aunt and an unborn baby she didn't want.

"The mother bound her body as tight as she could. She hoped the binding would suffocate her baby."

Minton's story brought two departed souls to life. I saw one struggling to enter the world, the other trying desperately to slam the door on him.

In spite of the mother's efforts, the baby was born—his body so twisted that he was crippled for life.

But, his spirit flew arrow-straight.

"He raised himself up from poverty to become a doctor," Minton told me. "Then he became Dean of The Arkansas University College of Medicine."

A baby whose entry was dreaded grew to become a healing caregiver.

What does it mean to tell a story the way Minton does? Stories told well hold a different power than those told in ordinary ways.

If you say, "This is about a crippled baby who became a doctor," you have told the facts, but you have not created what only great storytelling can—empathy and compassion.

These are the traits needed in Healing Hospitals. That is why Ms. Sparks sometimes joins me in spreading her work to the caregiving world. It is not only important *that* we tell our stories of caregiving, but the *way* we tell them is also crucial.

Your truest principles are born from your stories. All the rules in the world are not as effective in culture change as are the stories we report.

> *Your truest principles are born from your stories.*

Stories are like jokes. They give you a chance to "get it" on your own rather than having someone explain it to you.

If you want to move a caregiving culture from fear to Love, tell stories of loving care. Tell them every day in large meetings and small; in boardrooms and in nurse's stations; from the podium and by the patient's bed.

Let stories ring out from the hearts of caregivers and patients alike. For it is through stories that you touch Love's truth and expiate your own fear.

Story 2—A Tale of Transformation

His father was a surgeon. Mark took the same path. When I met him he was in his final year of residency.

The story Mark told to himself was that he was his father's son and would therefore be like him. There was one problem.

Mark's father had a terrible temper. He had already been required to attend the state medical association's program for anger management. If he failed to change his privileges at our hospital would be withdrawn.

Mark knew nothing about this. When he started copying the same behavior I called him into my office. "You're not going to graduate if you don't do something about the abusive way you are treating our nurses," I told him.

Mark was stunned. "I didn't think that mattered," he told me. "My dad blew up. I thought it was okay."

"You need to decide who *you* are," I said. "If your story is that you are a copy of your dad, you're in trouble."

Years later, Mark told me our conversation changed his life. "I was telling myself I was like my dad. I realized that didn't need to be true."

Stories as Metaphors

"Storytelling seems to be a natural reaction to illness," Anatole Broyard wrote as he was dying of a terminal illness. "People bleed stories, and I've become a blood bank of them."

Without stories you plod through life unheard and unhearing. "Stories are antibodies against illness and pain," Broyard continues, "Anything is better than an awful silent suffering… [Stories] are the most effective ways to keep our humanity alive."

What is your role in facilitating healing through storytelling? Broyard advises that "a sick person can make a story…out of his illness as a way of trying to detoxify it."

For example, Broyard imagined his sickness as traveling to a disturbed country. He thought of it "as a love affair with a demented woman who demanded things I had never done before."

Alternatively he imagined his cancer as being like moving out of his old, cozy house into a new one that was all windows. These stories acted as a tonic for him.

Cancer-afflicted children understand this power. They create the story that their chemotherapy acts like warriors attacking their tumors.

Further, art and poetry help us create our way out of the hard chapters in our lives.

Story 3—How The Mother Test Came from a Story

"Spirituality means waking up. Most people, even though they don't know it, are asleep."

Father Anthony de Mello

One of the sweetest experiences you had as a child probably began with four magic words: "Once upon a time…" It was so exciting for me that I even remember the way the "O" in the first word appeared large on the pages of the story books my mother opened before me.

Imagine how many stories you have heard and told since your childhood.

Dozens if not hundreds of stories fill your days because your take on the world is shaped by the stories you tell yourself. For example, do you wake up telling yourself the story that you don't like your job, or that your boss is a jerk, or that you would be happy if only you had a new car?

If you want to change your worldview, look at the stories you are telling yourself and others.

Rami Shapiro wrote in the book *Hasidic Tales: Annotated and Explained*, "The stories we tell ourselves about ourselves determine the quality of the selves we imagine we are. The stories we tell about others determine the quality of our relationships with them."

The Mother Test helps wake you up by giving you a tough challenge. The idea for it arose from an encounter that is now an important story. What is the test?   ***If your mother were a patient in your organization, would every single person give her the loving care you think she deserves?***

Most people skip over the definition of The Mother Test too fast. Yes, it is a variation on the Golden Rule. But in a complex caregiving setting, what does it mean for *every* employee to treat *every* patient the way you want your mother to be treated?

An orthopedic surgeon signaled the difficultly in understanding the importance of loving care during a discussion we had in a hospital I was leading. "This loving care stuff is nice," he told me, "but if a patient comes to me with a compound comminuted fracture of the tibia how does that help? The leg doesn't need loving care. It needs my skill."

"The leg is attached to the patient and the patient needs loving care," I answered.

What changed the conversation for me was that my response seemed to have no effect. This talented physician could not see the point until I took the discussion one step further.

"What if the patient is your mother?" I asked.

His response suggested an earthquake change in the story he told himself about his own caregiving. "Oh, well," he said, clearly startled, "if it was *my* mother then I would certainly want her to receive all the love in the world."

> *The Mother Test:*
> *If your mother were a patient in your organization, would every single person give her the loving care you think she deserves?*

The Mother Test was born in that moment. Every patient is someone's mother, father, sister, brother, child, friend. Every patient's humanity calls for love.

But, can hospitals ensure this kind of love from *every* caregiver *all* the time? The answer is that all of us are inclined to conform to the culture in which we live and work.

On the first day of kindergarten, we all look around to determine how we are supposed to behave. We take our clues from the teacher and our fellow classmates and act accordingly.

When you were new to your work environment you did the same thing. You looked around at your new work setting and observed your supervisor and your teammates.

If the culture tolerates mediocre care, it can be hard to sustain a personal standard of best care because your teammates are likely to give you a hard time.

This happened to my younger sister, a veteran receptionist at a large hospital selected as employee of the year for her loving caregiving. A supervisor called her in one day and said, "Martha, you need to stop getting down from your post to help people. You're overdoing it."

"But, I thought we were here to give the best care we could," Martha responded.

"Well, you are making the other employees look bad and I think you should stop that," the supervisor warned her.

If you want to grow cultures of loving care you and your supervisors must lead with love, not with fear and threats.

It is the responsibility of leaders to establish environments where loving care is celebrated, not frustrated. After all, the leader never knows when his or her own mother may need Radical Loving Care.

Story 4—The Housekeeper and the Old Man

"The divinity in each and every person can be witnessed and reached, only when you approach them as a faithful servant."

Vinoba Bhave

People often ask me to define Radical Loving Care. The short answer came to me from Deshaun, a member of the housekeeping staff at Baptist Hospital. "Loving care means helping other people no matter what," she told me while pushing her cart down the hallway.

Radical Loving Care means providing the best care all the time. When you are delivering Radical Loving Care you are an agent of Love's healing power.

Practicing Radical Loving Care doesn't usually look dramatic. Sacred Encounters (where Love meets need) occur every day.

This story of another housekeeper and an old man helps describe what Radical Loving Care looks like in a healthcare setting.

One day in 1998 I joined a group of caregivers for lunch. Each of them worked in environmental services.

"Let me ask you a question," Nadine, an eight year veteran, said to me. "Last night I was mopping the floor on the seventh floor. An old man was confused and he kept calling out for his daughter. I knew his daughter had already left. So I decided to take a chance." She hesitated.

"What kind of chance?" I asked.

"I looked down to the nursing station. Everyone was busy. So, I put down my mop, walked into the old man's room and held his hand. He calmed down real fast and soon he was asleep. So I went back out, picked up my mop and started cleaning the floor again. Is that what you call Radical Loving Care?"

"That's it," I was glad to affirm.

What was Nadine's risk? She might have drawn the ire of a passing supervisor. In the wrong kind of hospital, she might even have been "written up."

In the wrong setting a charge nurse might have scolded her with the warning that she should stick to mopping and direct care was the job of the nurses. Someone might even have warned her that if she did that pretty soon *everyone* would be doing it.

Of course, that's exactly what we want from the new RLC Teams—everyone making the extra effort to give loving care.

Other Ways Stories Teach

The story of the housekeeper and the old man became iconic at Baptist Hospital, even appearing on coffee mugs. We used it over and over to help supervisors and first line staff to understand that although rules are important, the *principle* that the patient comes first always trumps any rule.

We need the rules. In Healing Hospitals the staff knows when to break them to ensure that need is met with loving care—or to follow them to accomplish the same objective.

Story 5—Principles versus Rules

"It's not me. It's the law that wants you."

Inspector Javert to Jean Valjean in Victor Hugo's *Les Misérables*

Those familiar with Victor Hugo's classic story know that the character, Javert, relentlessly pursues Valjean for a trivial crime. His justification is only that "It's the law…" He gives no weight to humanity's law.

How many times have we heard a nurse or clerk or supervisor justify her or his position merely by saying, "It's policy."

It's not fear, but Love that wants us.

Professional staff members are bound by important protocols. They truly need to follow the rules in most situations.

In Healing Hospitals and other healthcare organizations, however, the members of RLC teams know when Love trumps the rules. In ordinary hospitals, things can go wrong when the rules are followed unthinkingly.

The Chief Nursing Officer at a Nashville hospice awoke one night struggling with acute pain. Her husband raced her to a large hospital ten minutes away.

His wife lay in the back seat as he pulled his car right up the Emergency room entrance and ran inside. "My wife is a nurse and she thinks she's dying," he shouted to the first caregiver he saw.

A nearby nurse grabbed a wheelchair and headed for the door. Her supervisor noticed.

"No wheelchairs outside the ER!" the supervisor shouted.

Fortunately, the nurse countermanded her boss. "I don't care what the rule is," she called out, "I have a patient out there who needs me."

Hospitals are often straight-jacketed by the flood of rules we impose to insure safe and legal operation. Nurses guided by Radical Loving Care understand how and when to ignore the rule in favor of the best care.

Story 6—Who Is Our Patient?

For doctors and first line caregivers, the answer to this question is easy. Sick people are their patients. For others in the system the answer may be subtle. For example, who is the leader's "patient?"

> *The number one job of leaders is to take care of the people who take care of people.*

My pathway into leadership of a Toledo hospital (formerly called Riverside) could not have begun in a more incongruous place. Prior to being named Vice President and General Counsel in 1975 I did not have a single bit of health care experience.

Instead, for the three years prior to entering the hospital world, I had been a prosecuting attorney with the U.S. Department of Justice. My daily challenge was winning convictions, not supervising caregiving. My client was "the people," as every prosecutor says in closing arguments.

On my first day of work, I was blunt with the department heads reporting to me. "I don't know anything about hospitals," I told the skeptical group, "I really need to count on each of you for your help."

They couldn't believe my lack of healthcare training. After all, how could their new boss be completely void of experience? I hoped my honesty would breed trust.

"The JCAHO (hospital accrediting body) is coming in two weeks," the Director of Planning told me.

"What's the JCAHO?" I asked.

"Wow," he answered. "You really *don't* know anything about hospitals, do you?"

The next day, I learned the answer to one of the most important questions *every* leader needs to ask: *Who is his or her "patient?"*

6

"Code Blue" —Taking Care of the People Who Take Care of People

S itting in my office, I heard a "Code Blue" paged over the PA system. Trained to help my clients in need, I immediately rose and started running toward the scene of the crisis.

Halfway down the hallway I stopped. *What was I supposed to do? Draft a will for a dying patient?*

I turned and walked back towards my office. *Who is my client?* I asked myself.

The answer came to me in a flash. The employees were my clients. My job was to take care of them.

This story led to a central principle practiced in all Healing Hospitals:

The number one job of leaders is to take care of the people who take care of people.

This principle encompasses every other. It means ensuring everything from good employee benefits and supportive leadership to secure financial condition. In other words, the sacred encounter for the leader comes through supporting the best possible relationships with the first line staff that are actually delivering care.

Story 7—The Actress/Doctor

> *Real compassion drives the highest competence because real compassion wants the best for the patient.*

Lunchtime is a great occasion to hear stories that teach about caregiving. In the doctor's dining room one day I sat next to a physician three years into her practice as an internist.

I asked her my favorite question: "How do you give loving care?"

She thought I was asking about compassion (instead of loving care which is both competence *and* compassion.) She looked at me the way caregivers sometimes do when approached by someone with no first line care experience.

"I start my rounds at 6:30 A.M.," she told me. "If I gave out compassion to every patient I'd be exhausted by noon. So I'm an actress. I pretend."

In fact, she was a first line caregiver. She was facing the daily demands of very sick people and I was not.

I had no business judging her decision to pretend compassion instead of suffering with it. In fact, she deserved compassion for everything she had to endure each day.

Still, I wondered which behavior would ultimately be more exhausting for her, pretending Love or living it?

Where is the balance between "professional" behavior that maintains distance and compassionate behavior that draws near? At one extreme, the doctor signals a lack of genuine caring. At the other, getting too close to patients may interfere with clinical judgment.

Obviously, we don't want a surgeon coming into the waiting area and telling the family what he or she may be thinking: "Oh God! The blood in there was terrible."

We also don't want this same surgeon approaching the family and getting melodramatic.

The finest caregivers provide answers. "The balance point moves," urologist Dr. Keith Hagan told me one day. "Because doctor's training is so heavily clinical I think each physician has to *nurture* compassion. Too many doctors are afraid of it. I lean to compassion because I know my clinical training will help me maintain professional balance."

Another veteran nurse told me, "I became a nurse because I believe in compassion. If I couldn't be compassionate in my work I'd be burned out."

Real compassion drives the highest competence because real compassion wants the best for the patient. This doesn't mean gushing.

It means loving with grace and skill.

Radical Loving Care (RLC) teams educate hearts as well as minds.

Story 8—The Energy in a "Calling"

After a meeting one day at Baptist Hospital I talked with two veteran obstetricians about what had drawn them to their work.

"I love delivering babies," the first one told me with light in his eyes. "It never gets old to me to see that baby come out, to help a new life enter the world, to see the joy in the mother's eyes. Of course, it's not always happy. But, if things start out wrong, I love the challenge of trying to make them right."

His partner turned to me with a flat expression. "I became an obstetrician because it was something I could do," he said. "That's pretty much it."

Both doctors had practiced for more than twenty-five years. One was still living his passion. The other was clearly burned out (in fact he later launched an unsuccessful effort to unionize his fellow physicians.)

The first doctor did not name his work as "a calling," but that's how it sounded to me. The second doctor clearly viewed his work as just a job.

The seeds of burnout are planted when we look at our work as daily drudgery. The best energy comes when we constantly renew our passion for caregiving.

Whether they use the word "calling" or not, RLC teams are populated by people who are passionate about their work.

Story 9—Deadre's Gift

Obviously, even the most passionate caregivers experience moments of fatigue. How has Deadre Hall, a nurse with more than thirty years' experience in Neuro-Intensive Care units, sustained her healing energy?

"Every morning on the way to work, I listen to music that inspires me," she told me.

"Every morning?" I asked.

"Yes. And I sit in my car in the parking lot until I think I'm ready to go in and give my best to my patients."

"How long does that energy last?" I asked.

"Sometimes for the whole shift and sometimes only ten minutes," she answered. "When I feel myself going negative, I step out of the unit and take a breath. That usually is all I need."

Deadre's daily ritual has helped make her one of the finest nurses I've ever encountered.

If you want to build an RLC Team, encourage each member to find a ritual that refreshes caregiving energy. Find one, as well, for the team to practice as a group.

Story 10—How Much Time Does Loving Care Take?

A failure to understand loving care causes some to say, "I don't have the time to do that."

How much time does it take?

When loving care is part of your daily practice, then that's what you are doing all the time.

Watching four groups of people wading through the cafeteria lines at Baptist Hospital one day, I noticed that the customers in the fastest lane often smiled as they encountered the cashier. The folks in the other three lines wore that dead expression we adopt when we're bored.

Lois Powers manned the cash register for the happy group. She had been doing it for twenty-five years.

"What your secret?" I asked.

"I tell jokes," she told me. "Hospitals are grim places. I find a new joke every day and try to brighten the moment."

She added an important caveat. "Of course, some people look too sad for a joke so when I see one I just touch their arm."

"What a wonderful thing for a cashier to do," I said.

"I'm not a cashier," she reminded me. "I'm a caregiver."

Cashiers make change. Caregivers create Sacred Encounters in as little as a few seconds.

Everyone in a healthcare organization is a caregiver.

Story 11—The Look of Loving Care

Among the most poignant scenes I've ever observed occurred one night in a neonatal intensive care unit. The first thing I saw when I entered the area during my rounds was a nurse stroking the back of the tiniest of babies.

Medical care has advanced to the point where infants as small as a pound or two can be saved. I asked Lisa, the nurse, how the baby was doing.

"This baby is dying right now. He's probably got only about another half an hour," she answered, as she continued to stroke his back.

"Where are the parents?"

"They were too upset to stay," she told me. "He will die with me."

There is nothing in the nursing manual or the standards of accreditation that require this kind of care. Lisa could easily have justified leaving this baby's side to attend to other patients who had a chance of recovery.

This baby could not ask for help. Neither could he thank Lisa for comforting him in his last moments on this earth.

This baby's life could not be saved. But, by opening her heart, Lisa gave him the gift of healing through Radical Loving Care.

Story 12—The Salad Lady

During a lunch to honor caregivers with twenty-five years of service I was seated next to a member of the dietary staff at Riverside Methodist Hospital.

"Congratulations on twenty-five years," I told her, impressed with her long dedication. "Where do you work?"

"I work in salads," she said with a stout-hearted smile.

"How long have you worked in salads?"

"Twenty-five years," she replied proudly.

Then, as if reading my mind, she quickly followed by saying, "I know it probably doesn't seem like much compared to your big job, but I love working in salads. I love thinking how all those nurses and techs and everybody will be coming to lunch and there will be my salad just waiting for them."

"Congratulations again," I told her. I was embarrassed that with her insightful recognition she had read my mind that I actually had been thinking about the contrast between her job and mine—that somehow because I got paid more and had a "big" title my work was somehow more important.

She was right. I was wrong.

Of course, she isn't *just* "The Salad Lady." She is a dedicated woman who, thank God, loves to prepare salads each day. Too many doing the same kind of work become bored and end up both hating their work and often doing a bad job.

It's strange how we pass judgment on the importance of different roles in caregiving settings. Our thoughts about that can leak into our language and our way of thinking about our fellow beings.

Too often, I have heard otherwise well-meaning executives refer to first line staff members as "the lower level employees." What they mean, I suppose, is the lower paid employees. But, it's a short step from lower paid to lower level and an even shorter step after that down the road to condescension.

7

Your New Story— Living Love, Not Fear

How do we learn to live love rather than spending our lives afraid? One way is to change our stories.

The most fascinating journey you can take is to create a new story around your life.

If you are a leader you can change the story of an entire organization.

The beginning of your "new story" adventure is to ask yourself questions: What parts of my story grow from Love? Which parts are informed by fear?

If you are the one who decides how you feel why are you choosing to live fear instead of Love?

At a personal level, you can begin by deciding what you want your days to be like right now.

Creating your new story can be as simple as Monday morning. It's part of America's work culture to hate Mondays.

Since there's going to be a Monday every seven days why fret about it? You can change your life story by deciding to celebrate Monday instead of dreading it.

Many people have never thought of their lives in this way. The process of doing so can lead to the finest awakening you may ever experience.

But, the process can only succeed if you are completely honest with yourself. The deeper you probe the greater your growth will be.

What is your story about your work as a caregiver? Do you think of yourself as both compassionate and competent?

Why did you become a caregiver? What are the influences that have shaped your decisions since then? Who is shaping them now, you or someone else?

Do you think of your job as hard labor or as a calling? Every job has tiresome elements. If these aspects dominate your tale it's time to consider a new story.

Do you tell yourself it's your supervisor's fault? Do you blame your team?

What is the story of your work culture? What can you contribute to help change that culture so that caregiving becomes more of a joy?

It's hard to do this work alone. Group sessions with fellow workers or friends are crucial.

The stories you tell yourself and the way you tell them impact your world every day. *Change your stories and you change your life. Change your hospital's stories, and you change the lives of all who work and receive care there.*

If you are a leader, change the story of the culture and you will change the lives of the caregivers you supervise. If the story of your culture tolerates mediocrity, then mediocrity becomes your culture's truth.

If the story becomes *we are a culture of caring*, then that impacts the behavior of every caregiver and every patient every day.

Imagine the impact that would have on patient care.

8

Are You Tolerating Substandard Care?

R emember: *If you are a leader of any kind, do you work with anyone you would not want caring for your own mother?* If so, why are they working for you? What are you going to do to either retrain that individual or remove them? What are you doing to recognize and reward the caregivers who pass The Mother Test all the time?

The bottom line is that if we want patients to be treated with loving care we need to hire and nurture caregivers and leaders who will give such care. To do that requires growing cultures of loving care that will support the best!

Culture is king. Loving cultures, like gorgeous gardens, must be nourished every day. The work never stops.

Successful gardeners know what it takes. When a storm comes, they don't surrender. When weeds invade the garden they pull them out. When infestation comes they drive it away.

Healthy cultures need strong and persistent support. Their success also requires an understanding that the core energy in a garden comes from Love's sun and rain. The role of the leader is to support loving care so that healing cultures may be sustained.

9

Change Strategies—The New Radical Loving Care (RLC) Teams

"...I learned at last what it means to love people and why love is worn down by loneliness, pity, and anger."

Czeslaw Milosz

Y ou have seen teams self-destruct because of the way some members are afflicted with "loneliness, pity and anger."

You may even have been a member of a **Toxic Team**—one where members break into factions and focus more on sabotaging each other than they do on patient care. The primary responsibility for converting a toxic team to a healthy one rests with the team leader.

Every team tells itself a story about who they are. The story shapes the team's reality.

> *It's a nightmare to be part of a toxic team. It's an everyday joy to work on a healthy team that celebrates caring by supporting each other in the sacred work of caregiving.*

Eckhart Tolle teaches us that the ego always takes things personally. Our egos accumulate insults as wounds, many of which never heal. You are not your ego, Tolle writes. You can overcome your sense of anger and self-pity by stepping back from your ego and observing what is happening. This is both a path to healing and a terrific exercise for team members in learning how to participate in healthy teams focused on patients.

Lists of steps are not the best ways to learn Love because they suggest that merely walking through the steps will, by itself, create a new culture of caring. Radical Loving Care lies deeper than surface steps. Still, there are guideposts that can be helpful.

Radical Loving Care (RLC) teams make organization-wide change do-able.

Some teams are already passing The Mother Test. How do you ensure that every team is accomplishing this goal?

There are steps to follow and criteria to establish to determine if teams are reaching RLC team status. Imagine the impact on the hospital's culture when every team arrives at this level.

First, each team leader and caregiver needs to understand the role of compassion and how it integrates with highest caregiver competence to become Radical Loving Care.

It's a nightmare to be part of a toxic team. It's a an everyday joy to work on a healthy team that celebrates caring by supporting each other in the sacred work of caregiving.

The Challenge of Compassion with Competence

"Wanting to alleviate pain without sharing it is like wanting to save a child from a burning house without the risk of being hurt."

Henri Nouwen

On a recent windless day I watched several jets accumulate cloudy tracks that intersected far up in the sky. As I raised my camera to photograph the phenomenon I thought of the people on those planes, their energies crisscrossing in their temporary communities like invisible contrails.

It requires courage to show up for life—to find the intersection between our soul and the soul of another.

Beauty glows at intersections. Isn't this the appeal of the image of the Christian cross? We are drawn to the nexus of a naked cross, not to the edges.

Compassion rises in waves from the ocean of Love. Her crests may lead to troughs of fatigue (and sometimes fear.) Compassion is the human expression of Love's eternal energy.

Human energy ebbs and flows. Love is constant.

Many of us used to be present to suffering but it became too painful. We are always running the risk of being hurt in the course of our caregiving just as we may have been hurt elsewhere in our lives. Henri Nouwen understands this.

"Those who do not run away from our pains but touch them with compassion bring healing and new strength," Nouwen wrote.

But, each of us carries scars. Pain has taught us to be wary.

The Santa Trick

As children some of us showed up for Christmas until we found out there was no Santa. After that, if we showed up, we may have appeared with a new reluctance to be fully present lest we be tricked again.

After I got "The Santa Disclosure" at about age seven, I immediately wondered about God. If Santa was a fake, was God another trick played by adults? Not until I began to think of God as Love could I overcome my cynicism.

The reason it is so important for caregivers to establish real presence with patients is that it is the only way to truly appreciate the patient's needs. Is this difficult? Of course it is. It is worth doing only if you are genuinely interested in meeting those needs.

The Crucial Intersection of Compassion with Competence

If we truly care about those in pain we will work to change how we *define* them. The more we imagine the other as a stranger, the more we may dissect that person away from our hearts as not worthy of our compassion (as if compassion were a finite quantity that might run out.)

The challenge is that *compassion requires empathy* and *competence suggests a need for professional distance.* Professionals are not supposed to care for members of their own families and yet it is those members for whom we want the deepest compassion.

In fact, I have seen professionals give spectacular care to their own children and to friends of theirs who are, in many cases, closer to them than family. So the family/professionalism dichotomy, while understandable, is false.

The challenge of compassion is, as King said, to be as "tough-minded" with those we love as we are "tender-hearted."

Who are We?

"I am not a mechanism, an assembly of various sections," D.H. Lawrence wrote in his poem *Healing.* "It is not [only] because the mechanism is working wrongly, that I am ill. I am ill because of wounds to the soul, to the deep emotional self...."

How do caregivers reach this "deep emotional self" that has been wounded? It's impossible to develop compassion for patients until we have first found it for ourselves.

In the same way that caregiving requires both compassion and competence, those who have found *self*-compassion sometimes need professional help in order to develop the *self-competence* to treat their own pain.

It is crucial that we distinguish pity from compassion. There's a silly-sounding rhyme that describes the critical difference: "Pity stops and stares. Compassion stoops and cares."

Self-pity is an ugly thing and can cause depression. Compassion is beautiful and lives at the heart of our healing.

Everyone one of us has suffered enormous personal pain. Can we develop compassion for our pain instead of pity? After that, do we have both the strength and the competence to enter the pain of another and, in so doing, relieve it?

If this is not loving care, what is?

Interestingly, it's not hard to teach pity for others. Pity appeals to our ego's desire to be superior. If I pity you that means I elevate myself to a superior position and delegate you to an inferior one.

The same is true with self-pity. That's why we may wallow in it in an effort to draw the sympathy of others.

True compassion reminds us that what we want from others during our own pain is presence. Presence may not feel like enough, but it is a precious gift currently withheld (unintentionally) from most patients by task-obsessed caregivers who feel they don't have the time for what one doctor described to me as "that compassion stuff."

Compassion is not separate from the performance of tasks. It is integral to the successful performance of curing as well as healing.

Love In The Moment

"I'm planning to give loving care during my shift tonight," a caregiver told me recently. It's the peak of noble thoughts and exactly the kind of thing everyone in need at that time wants to hear. There's a related thought. It's not about what I'm *planning* to do but what I am *doing* right now.

Frequently, I find myself plotting new ways to live Love. What matters, of course, is not what I am intending in the future or ruing about the past but what I am doing right now.

Sitting at my computer (imagining you at yours) I am living love by pausing to send up a prayer for a man who, now age eighty, is ill and tired of life, and another prayer for a woman who, in this moment, is suffering with cancer knowing that it may soon take her life.

How can a doctor or nurse respond to a patient's anger when they, as caregivers, are late responding to the patient's need? A frequent response is, "Well, I was busy taking care of other patients" or, worse, "We're short staffed today" or "My partner called in sick."

The problem with these answers is that the patient can do nothing about these excuses—and may well be made more uncomfortable knowing there are not enough people to care for patients.

The better response has to do with giving love NOW: "I'm so sorry to be slow responding. That must have been hard for you. I'm here now. How may I help you."

The love we give now is more important and any we plan for tomorrow. Tomorrow, of course, will be another set of "nows." For "now" is the only time we have

Can We Teach Compassion?

Compassion cannot be taught using conventional teaching methods. This is because compassion is not a set of steps.

My friend, Olivia McIvor touches this challenge in her book, *Turning Compassion Into Action*. She writes that compassion is better "caught than taught."

Doctors and nurses who are taught through memorization and the learning of procedures may be stumped by this truth. As a result, compassion, like Love, is quickly dismissed as something that can't be taught. "You either have it or you don't," some say.

The reason this statement is false is that we all have the capacity to express compassion. Once you understand that pity and compassion are opposites, you can begin to understand that your ability to express compassion for others stems from your ability to develop compassion for yourself.

Do you experience empathy with the pain you have suffered? If so, then you can transfer your understanding to an expression of love for others?

There is, of course, a moment when compassion can run so deep that it can disable us from delivering the kind of care the patient needs. There is also a phenomenon known as Compassion Fatigue.

Caregivers can help each other identify when this is occurring. The solution, however, is *not* to turn away from giving compassion because it sometimes wears you out. The answer is to let the experience of fatigue teach you how to keep your caregiving in balance.

Radical Loving Care (RLC) Teams & Compassion

Healthcare organizations establish teams of people who, at first, don't know each other. Teams, by definition, are assembled to do something.

What if your unit was a super team? In health care settings seeking to change cultures using an RLC Team, the concept *compassionate presence* is learned in small groups. The leader does not "teach" it. Instead, the leader facilitates, providing an atmosphere that allows caregivers to learn their own gifts of loving care.

The best way to do this is, again, through storytelling.

Donna Gares, CEO at the San Jacinto Hospital (part of Houston-based Methodist Health System) uses stories with classic effectiveness. She always begins staff meetings with members standing to recite a story. Why does this matter? It matters because the stories report episodes of healing behavior in the organization. Because of the stories, everyone in the organization understands the concept and practice of Radical Loving Care. You feel it the moment you walk in the door.

Every member of the group takes the cue from Donna that these are the stories that matter—*this* is the priority.

This is one reason Donna has been so effective in advancing a culture of loving care.

Storytelling signals the cultural values of any group. When stories celebrate the delivery of compassion, caregivers learn firstly that compassion is an important value for the entire group, and secondly, they learn what their own caregiving would look like if they expressed greater compassion towards their patients.

Consider the two-thousand-year-old power of the parable of the Good Samaritan. The priest in the story may have pitied the wounded man fallen by the side of the road, but it is the Good Samaritan who shows us what compassion looks like.

We can copy the Good Samaritan's actions, but does that necessarily mean we "feel" love for the person we are helping? Does it matter?

Yes. It is the compassion you have for the other that informs your decisions about what to do. If you lack compassion, you might either stop short of giving all the help that is needed or you may actually overdo your service in ways that irritate the patient.

Next time you encounter anyone in pain consider the quality of your compassion. What does it look like? If you had to paint it what colors would you use? How does it sound, as music? What is its fabric?

If you had to tell a story about how you give compassion how would it go?

The point of this exercise is to help the caregiver understand what might be missing as well as what is there.

Cultures of Compassion

Culture changes through people.

Look in the mirror. Is your Servant's Heart beating?

Organizations change through teams.

Next, look at your fellow caregivers. Do you want them taking care of *your* mother?

How would you bring about change?

10

Practices & Change Steps

I don't like listing steps because often lists don't touch the spiritual change needed to succeed. Still, team leaders need to take the following kinds of actions to build the culture of loving care that will transform their group to an RLC team.

1. Hire for A Servant's Heart

Everyone I've ever worked with seems to know what I mean by "A Servant's Heart." The way you hire one is to ask yourself during every employment interview: "Does the person before me have a Servant's Heart? If not, do they have the potential to develop one?"

One of the ways to find this out is to ask every prospect the most powerful question I've ever known: "How do you give loving care?" Most people have never been asked this question. It's understandable that they may be taken off guard. Give them a chance to tell you.

There are several advantages to a question like this. First, you get an insight from how the prospect responds. Some people say, "I don't know, I just do it." This beginning is okay but the inquiry should go deeper. People with a Servant's Heart can usually do this.

The second advantage is that this question signals to the potential new employee that Love is central to your culture.

Finally, staff members who ask this kind of question hear the echo of their question in their own lives. This reinforces the notion of Love in the heart of the interviewer.

Look at hiring practices. Are your team members engaged in "resume hiring?" Is their primary goal to fill a vacancy with a "warm body?" If so, change will never occur.

2. Orient with the IIF (Information, Inspiration, and Fun) Strategy

It was mid-morning when I rose to speak to about fifty new employees during my first week as CEO of Baptist Hospital. Looking out at the audience, I immediately noticed that four new employees were sound asleep.

In speeches and seminars I've posed this situation and asked what I should have done. One leader suggested I fire all four of them.

Now there's an idea. "Wake up, you're fired." Then tell the other new employees, "Welcome to the new world of Radical Loving Care."

The problem is *not* those four sleepy employees. They may have just finished a double shift or simply had a hard time sleeping during the night (one person told me there had been gunshots and sirens in her neighborhood all night.)

The issue is that orientations are boring. They are designed as information dumps.

This is one of the easiest areas to correct.

The IIF strategy adds two key additional elements to information: inspiration and fun.

For example: At Baptist Hospital one of our human resources managers actually mounted a disco ball in the middle of the auditorium, hung crepe paper and greeted new employees with the sounds of Aretha Franklin singing "RESPECT" over the PA system. New employees loved it. Right away, it signaled they were in a special place.

We are all more receptive to inspiration if it's mixed with humor. 1) Find the most inspiring speakers in the organization and have them present, whether they are part of HR or not. 2) Ask existing speakers to rethink their standard speeches to add elements that inspire. 3) Use the concept of the Golden Thread to let new staff know they are part of a long tradition of caregiving. 4) Be sure and let them know that *everyone is a caregiver*, not just nurses and therapist.

How do you make the boring stuff interesting? Our HR team at Baptist designed games the staff could play to help them enjoy learning about benefits.

In other words, be creative. Don't settle for doing things the way they've always been done. Every organization can improve orientation. Start practicing the IIF strategy today.

3. Add the Servant's Heart Criteria to Employee Reviews and Training.

It's not enough to improve hiring and orientation. If a new employee leaves an inspiring orientation and is greeted by a negative supervisor and a demoralized team they will be even more discouraged than if you had done nothing.

The concepts of Radical Loving Care must be reinforced organization wide. Train staff to consider the big question every day "How am *I* giving loving care?" or "How did *I* do giving loving care to my patients, my fellow staff, myself."

Teach staff the five relationships. Design staff meetings to allow team members to tell stories of success.

4. Use Positive Language

Most of us are raised in environments where we are constantly told what *not* to do. RLC teams always focus on what *to* do, not what to avoid.

When we are told not to eat certain foods, it makes those foods more appealing and harder to resist. Smokers who are told to quit have a hard time succeeding if they think in the negative.

When the brain hears "Don't Smoke" it immediately thinks about the appeal of smoking. When the mind is told "stay healthy" then quitting smoking becomes easier.

Say to a basketball player on the free throw line, "Don't miss," and you've increased his or her chances of blowing the shot. Tell a nurse she or he better not make a medication error and the error rate will rise.

Staff members who are encouraged to make sure they are always giving the right medications are much less likely to make medication errors than those who are warned not to make them. The "not" word introduces a negative thought pattern. If I am thinking what "not" to do, I automatically think of the mistake I am trying not to make.

Train staff to use positive language. Start by using it yourself.

5. Practice Tough-Minded, Tender-Hearted Leadership

Most leaders at all levels have trouble determining how "close" their relationship should be to the people they supervise. The first step in determining the right balance is to ask where you are right now.

Do you know anything about the families of your staff? Do you know what they like to do when they are not at work?

Strict leaders worry about being taken advantage of. They imagine their role as a sort of drill sergeant whose job is to keep the staff in line.

Over-nice leaders want everyone to like them. They are loath to impose discipline and fear angry reactions.

Both approaches are grounded in fear, not love, and both fail. The strict leader generates fear and the approach causes mistakes and staff resistance. The overly-nice leader may generate team sloppiness.

6. Show Appreciation & Encourage

Show me an RLC team and I will show you a group that is constantly encouraging each other as well as expressing appreciation for each other.

Other teams engage in blaming. RLC teams take responsibility and work for improvement.

The medical staff at Scottsdale Healthcare System hit on an approach that seems obvious and yet was not. They encouraged doctors to approach nurses and other team members and to thank them for taking care of their patients.

It was done and it worked. If you want patients to receive better care, encourage the behavior you want to see practiced. Thank those who are practicing.

It's simple and it works.

7. Make Positive Use of Rounding

The loving leadership principle in rounding follows the positive language track. If you only ask staff questions like "did you get your charts done" or "are you hitting your budget" then you are signaling that these are your sole priorities.

If, as you make your rounds, you ask your staff how they are giving loving care, then you suggest Love is the core value. Treat staff like the adults they are. Harassing them about charts and budgets is like asking teenagers if they have their homework done.

The basics should be assumed. Errant caregivers know their weaknesses. If charts are not being done, ask "How may I help" rather than using threats.

8. Respect for *People* Wearing Patient Gowns

No one wants to come to a hospital. Who says on Saturday night, "I know what we can do for fun—let's check into a hospital."

In my first weeks working in hospitals (after practicing law for seven years) I was amazed to notice how demeaned we are when we don a patient gown. Naturally, those things look ridiculous. In fact, during my years as CEO at Riverside Methodist Hospital we tried hard to find a new design.

One day, we came up with the best answer. It is founded in respect, not in design.

We needed to help our caregivers understand that the most important uniform in the hospital is not the surgeon's scrubs or a coat and tie, but the *patient gown*.

The gown tells us why we are there. Its wearers are suffering and need our respect, not our derision.

9. Use the Language of Caregiving

Along with treating those wearing patient gowns with respect is language that demonstrates the same virtue. I have heard emergency room patients referred to as "frequent flyers," orthopedic patients as "knees" and surgical patients by their diagnosis. So the patient in Room 4005 becomes "The Gall Bladder" rather than the person with that disease.

So what? The problem with this kind of language is not only that it demeans the patient but it also degrades the caregivers. We are treating people who have diseases, not diseases with people attached to them.

If I refer to a disoriented patient as "The Screamer" then I unintentionally signal that that individual is less of a person. The label can even cause that patient to be ignored.

A radiologic technologist told me one day that he was just a "button pusher." If he really believes that, than his work has become just a job, not a calling.

RLC team members don't want *their* mothers X-rayed by "button pushers." They want loving caregivers.

Language affects the entire healing process. Teams that engage in the language of respect are supporting loving care.

10. Make Simple Changes through Piloting Simple Ideas

Broad, simple concepts like Radical Loving Care need to be broken down into simple ideas you can execute right away. Here are some examples. These are obviously wise steps. You know you are in the right culture when these steps become natural.

Here are some examples of the kind of loving care that is fostered in Healing Healthcare settings:

Code Team Pauses—A Harvard-trained physician noticed that code teams worked with incredible effectiveness while the patient was still alive. If the patient died, she saw that the team quickly dispersed, as if their work, and the patient they were looking after, no longer mattered. She initiated the following new practice.

If a patient died during a code, the head of the team would ask everyone to please "Pause for ten seconds to honor the life of this patient."

This practice creates an instant Sacred Encounter by affirming the humanity of all concerned. The idea is simple. Everyone likes it. Can you make this happen in your organization?

Healing Language—At Nashville's Baptist Hospital, an admitting clerk had a beautiful idea. "When patients come to my desk, I never start by telling them to sign in. If they are in pain, I acknowledge that by saying something like, 'I'm sorry to see you're in pain.' If they are anxious, I try to give them my personal reassurance before I give them any instructions."

This kind of change involves a few brief sentences. It doesn't require re-drafting any policy manuals, either.

One-Page Personal Histories—While jogging, Hospital Chief Operating Officer Doreen Dan's husband was critically injured. When she reached the hospital where he was taken she discovered the staff did not know his name (he had been wearing no identification) and had classified him as a John Doe. She immediately prepared a one-page history to let staff know personal facts about her husband. She understood how critical it is that staff members know patients as human beings.

Doreen didn't stop there. She initiated the practice of one-page personal histories to be added to each patient chart as part of nursing practice.

Touch Cards—How do we keep ourselves refreshed and renewed with each new patient? At Mercy Gilbert Hospital in Arizona, CEO Laurie Eberst got her teams to design touch-cards to be placed at the entrance to each patient room. The idea was that staff members would pause for a second and touch the card before entering a room at the same time they hit the hand cleanser at the door. The cards carry words like "Pause, Reflect, Heal."

The Everyday Thank You—Physicians at Scottsdale Health System are establishing a practice of asking doctors to thank nurse staff members every day for the work they are doing to care for the patients. That's all. But, it's more than happens in most care settings.

Blessing-of-the-Hands Ceremonies—These ceremonies are conducted regularly in the Catholic hospitals led by CEO Laurie Eberst. She knows that rituals reinforce values and how they are lived. In the ceremony, each caregiver's hands are blessed as a way of signifying one of the most important ways caregivers heal—with their hands.

Navigators—At Parrish Medical Center, CEO George Mikitarian wants to carry the welcome to new employees beyond the orientation ceremony. Veteran employees are selected as Navigators and each one is teamed up with a new employee to help further introduce them to the Radical Loving Care culture at Parrish.

11

Loving Leadership

R adical Loving Care is not to be discounted as a bunch of "touchy-feely" nonsense. Watch out for people who refer to Love in this way. To demean it with such language is to deny to *all* people in hospitals the gift of Love's presence.

There is nothing loving about caregivers who deliver compassion without competence. There is nothing loving about delivering substandard care and trying to cover it by being nice. Do you really want someone caring for *your* mother who is nice but incompetent?

The concept of the Healing Hospital is grounded in Radical Loving Care. Leaders have introduced it in hundreds of hospitals. Loving leaders in the best caregiving organizations have figured out (or are focused on figuring out) how to build these cultures so powerfully that *every* patient encounter is treated as sacred.

Don't let anyone tell you their organization is too big to develop a culture that lives Love every day and night.

Working with First Line Staff

A year or two into my twelve-year term as President and CEO of Riverside Methodist Hospital in Columbus, it occurred to me that I needed to do more to be present for the first line staff. If I was going to be a leader who celebrated the caregiver-to-patient relationship, I needed to spend less time in my office and in meetings distant from caregiving, and more time with the actual caregivers.

We had nearly six thousand employees and more than a thousand doctors on staff in our thousand-bed hospital. I decided to spend most of one eight-hour shift each month working in a different department.

Ten years later, up until the day I left Riverside, I was still doing it. Long after I left, I'm still being told that work built morale as much as any other single thing we did.

Most leaders (including me) will never understand (unless they started out that way) what it's like to work in housekeeping every day or to deliver care to patients. Also, it is very important not to engage in this approach unless you are ready to make a significant commitment. Working fifteen minutes in a department and getting your picture taken for the hospital newspaper looks cynical and will breed distrust instead of support. But, if you believe in the power of understanding someone else by "walking in her or his shoes" then I encourage you, as a leader, to find ways to do this.

Although a number of my fellow leaders tried my approach, I didn't insist on it and it is not for every leader. You have to believe in the power of the example this kind of action represents.

The first steps are difficult. It's humbling for lots of CEOs to trade a business suit for a housekeeping uniform. It's strange to find yourself folding sheets in the hospital laundry, washing dishes in the back room of the cafeteria, or pushing a portable X-ray machine down the hallway.

The apparent role change can throw people. "Hey, will you empty my waste basket?" one uneasy director asked me the first time she saw me in uniform. "Sure," I answered, quieting her for the time being.

"What are you doing in that silly outfit?" a surgeon said to me when he saw me in a housekeeping uniform. Another housekeeping caregiver was standing next to me. I walked the physician away from the scene. "Doctor," I told him, "that fellow with me wears this 'silly' outfit every day. He's the one who keeps your operating room clean. Help me show him his job is important."

The doctor walked back to the housekeeper, apologized, and thanked him for his work.

And there are other, sometimes funny, hazards to fellow staff.

After several months of working with them, the first line staff began to trust that I really respected their work. Several years later during an organizing attempt by our Radiology Department, other leaders and I were able to use our credibility to dissolve their drive.

The department engaged in a work stoppage threatening care throughout the hospital. When they asked to meet with me on a Sunday I knew some of them would be coming in from home and they would bring their kids. Against our labor lawyer's advice, I went to the meeting. In addition, I brought my teenage daughter with me.

It was a big help that all the staff already knew me and many had seen me working in their department. In other words, they knew they could trust me.

Within twenty-four hours, all but two of the fifty employees were back at work. The threat never returned.

Dishwashing, Humor & Humility

A funny thing happened when I began my program of working on the front lines in Nashville. As I stood beside Daryl washing dishes at Baptist Hospital, I found myself entertaining some arrogant thoughts. *"What a great leader I am,"* I said to myself. *"Here I am with my arms up to my elbows in piping hot water when I could be clean and dry in my fancy office."*

"What do you like best about this job?" I asked Daryl, an eleven-year veteran of the dish-room.

Daryl scanned the pans I'd been washing, some of which I'd put in the wrong spot. His response put me in my place. "Mr. Chapman, what I like most is working alone!"

Example & Presence

Shortly after our son was born in 1968, I asked our minister if he could give me some pointers to help me be a good father. "Could I make a series of appointments with you?" I asked.

Sure, we can do that," he answered. "We could spend hours discussing what it means to be a good father. But, I can give you the answer in two words. The first one is "example." Set a good one and you've done at least half of your job."

"What's the second?" I asked, thinking this teaching might be more painless than I thought.

"I'll tell you in a few weeks," he said. "Meanwhile, think about that first word."

I did as he asked, reflecting on what it meant to signal values by behavior, beyond words. Every parent wants to instruct. Teaching by example is what works best.

A few weeks later, the minister revealed the other word. "Presence," he said with a twinkle in his eye.

"Presence?" I asked anxiously. "But, I'm a busy young lawyer. I can't be there all the time."

"You don't have to be there all the time. But, when you are there be fully present. Don't be looking over your son's head at the television or talking to someone else on the phone. Show up for him!"

As you can see, this two-word teaching has stayed with me all this time. I'm glad to say that both of our children have grown up to be wonderful adults and parents themselves.

Every leader tells the front line staff that they matter. Too often, however, leaders distance themselves from the team that delivers care. In other words, they show up for board members but they don't show up for employees. They think they are setting a good example; instead, they may be living in terms of the language I heard from one CEO. Discussing a need to reduce staff, he said, "How many bodies do we have to toss out?"

The Chief Financial Officer, following this example, responded in kind. "We'll have to cut about thirty-seven units of expense," he answered.

When top leaders refer to caregivers as "bodies" and "units of expense" it signals to everyone that employees are somehow less than human.

Contrast that with the following sterling examples set by some of the top leaders at America's Healing Hospitals.

Examples of Living Loving Leadership

"The Mayo Way" & Radical Loving Care at the Cleveland Clinic

Consider the consistency of care in the **Mayo Clinic**. The culture in that organization is so strong that the staff there proudly refers to their approach as "The Mayo Way."

At the renowned Cleveland Clinic, Chief Experience Officer **Bridget Duffy, M.D.** (with the full blessing of The Clinic's President) introduced culture change to strengthen the system's quality of care. Part of the change she led included the introduction of the Radical Loving Care concept and the Healing Hospital approach.

Both the Mayo and Cleveland clinic systems are staffed by hundreds of doctors. The idea of culture change seemed impossible. But, look at the trend of patient satisfaction scores and top rankings that both these organizations have sustained and you will see the power of loving care in action.

George Mikitarian

The first leader named as Healing Hospital CEO of the Year was **Dr. George Mikitarian**. George is a prime example of Martin Luther King's "tough-minded, tender-hearted" leadership style. He has taken **Parrish Medical Center** to the top of the Radical Loving Care scale by transforming a culture that was average and leading it to excellence.

How did George do it? First, he and his team engaged an understanding of the key principles of this new approach. Second, they began to weave a healing quilt from their existing staff and environment into a coherent strategy for Parrish.

"I don't mind copying wisdom from others," George told me. Of course, following the wisdom of others is itself a sophisticated kind of wisdom.

In a stellar and sustained display of courage, George stood his ground against a group of doctors bent on sabotaging the new initiatives. Status quo caregivers hate it when they are challenged to move to a higher level because some know they can't make it.

George knew the rest of the hospital staff was checking to see if he and the board would have the courage to remove the privileges of one particularly errant physician. When the doctor was ejected from the medical staff everyone in the hospital knew that leadership was serious about establishing a Healing Hospital.

And that is exactly what happened (and is happening) at Parrish Medical Center. They got serious and they have sustained the loving care effort across several years now. They understand that you can't "install" loving care. You have to grow it and then you have to nurture it. The journey is continuous and never ends.

Laurie Eberst

Laurie Eberst is a pioneer of the Healing Hospital movement in the west. When she began as CEO of **Mercy Gilbert Hospital** in Arizona there was no building and no staff.

Laurie, a former Chief Nursing Officer, took the Radical Loving Care concept to heart. She literally built the entire organization on its foundation. The building design became one of the finest environments for healing in the country.

But, Laurie, like George, knew that a successful hospital is made from much more than bricks and mortar. She hired the staff using Healing Hospital principles: "We only want people with a Servant's Heart," she said.

Another one of Laurie's fine decisions was to hire **Kim Wilson** (currently Chief Operating Officer at St. John's Regional Medical Center, Oxnard) as Chief Nursing Officer at Mercy Gilbert. After the staff was assembled, Laurie did another brilliant thing. She established a director position responsible for overseeing cultural development and hired the wonderful **Grace Ibe** for the job.

These three succeeded so well that Laurie was promoted to President and CEO of the (now) three-hospital St. John's Healthcare system (part of Dignity Health) based in Oxnard, California. As of this writing, the organization is becoming another thriving example of a healing organization.

Patrick Taylor, M.D.,

As a young boy growing up in Florida, **Pat Taylor** wanted to be an astronaut. An excellent student, he progressed through high school rapidly approaching his dream.

The next step in his journey was the Air Force Academy. He secured the necessary appointment from a U.S. Senator.

All that was left was a routine physical.

Days after the physical exam, he received a surprising note. He had failed the rigorous physical test not because of a major problem but because of an orthopedic problem so minor he didn't know he had it.

Millions of us have scoliosis. It doesn't get in the way of our regular lives. But if you want to get into the Air Force Academy it's an automatic disqualifier.

His dreams of becoming an astronaut dashed, Pat wondered what to do next. During one of his summers at Notre Dame, he got a position as a hospital orderly. He loved it.

Duke Medical School came next followed by successful residencies at two more prestigious training programs.

"I was drawn to work in emergency medicine," Dr. Taylor told me. "One reason may have been that I noticed that I was calm and clear-headed in the midst of chaos."

In his years of practice, Pat learned he was also good at business. In the course of earning his Masters, he discovered something else. He needed to practice his skills in team settings.

"Doctors don't receive much training for leadership in teams," Pat shared. "As a doctor, everyone looks to you to make the call."

As he had in other areas, Dr. Taylor developed his leadership team skills so well that he became President and CEO of **Holy Cross Hospital** in Fort Lauderdale. There, he has been working hard at developing a culture of loving care among the three thousand employees and physicians on staff.

"Attention to matters of the soul is crucial in a non-profit Catholic hospital," Pat says. "That's very important to me. It's at the core of my being."

How does a leader integrate a compassionate soul with the rigorous demands of leadership in a hospital setting?

Dr. Taylor offers a fascinating metaphor based on his fluency in Spanish. "When I was first learning another language, I would hear the Spanish sentence and translate it into the English I already knew. After awhile, I didn't need to take that step. Speaking Spanish became natural."

This is how he believes tough-minded caregivers can learn compassion. When they first practice it, they have to translate it through the language of competence they already know. After regular use, the practice of compassion with competence becomes natural.

Dr. Taylor's leadership team has been particularly effective at implementing the use of The Mother Test. This success was visible one afternoon when I was talking with Taren Johnson, a key nursing leader at Holy Cross. She was interrupted by a call, and after she hung up, I continued talking.

"Wait," she told me heading out the door. "Someone's mother needs me!"

Moving from his young-boy dreams to be an astronaut to his adult career practicing his calling as a physician-CEO, Dr. Patrick Taylor has become a successful example of Radical Loving Care. Every day and night, he strives to live his calling to be a loving leader.

Finance & Compassion: Chris Siebenaler

Leaders with backgrounds in finance often get a bad rap. Some think they don't understand the importance of compassion.

That's certainly not true of **Chris Siebenaler**, CEO of **Sugarland Hospital**, part of the highly-ranked Methodist Healthcare System based in Houston. Chris started his career in accounting and rose to successful leadership because he appreciated the balance of *compassion with competence*.

Finance helped Chris see one part of the equation. His role as a CEO helped him see the whole picture and how he could affect it.

Chris humbly acknowledges the mentorship of his colleague, **Donna Gares**, CEO at the **San Jacinto** campus of the Methodist system. Donna was an early advocate of Radical Loving Care and helped Chris further appreciate the values they both shared.

When I spoke with Chris during a trip to his organization, I learned part of the impact his father had on his leadership style.

"When I visited my dad in his leadership role with a company," Chris told me, "I noticed how good he was at relating to the first line staff. I could see the positive effect this had. When I moved into a leadership role, I practiced the same approach."

Chris has been so effective that the hospital he leads is thriving. Sugarland Methodist is a profile of diversity with a significant percentage of staff members from many different countries.

Chris knows how to meld these diverse cultures by helping everyone focus on the same core values. When you're admitted to Sugarland Methodist, you can expect caregiving that honors The Mother Test.

Fortunately, Chris is also chairing a system-wide committee to advance consistency in the culture of caring for the Methodist Healthcare System. Sometimes committees don't matter. This one does.

Leadership sets the tone. And the tone at Sugarland honors Radical Loving Care for all.

Jason Barker

Jason Barker knows how to hit organizational "home runs." He's done it twice with hospitals in regions as diverse as Southern California and Montana. Like **Laurie Eberst**, who did the same thing in markets in Arizona and California, Jason takes excellence with him wherever he goes. The result is peak performance.

Like **Chris Siebenthaler**, Jason is a former CFO who brings a remarkable sense of compassion to his role as a CEO. At St. Mary's in the St. Joseph Health System, Jason built a culture of compassion and competence that lifted his organization to new levels of performance.

At St. Vincent's in Billings, Jason has done something even more remarkable. Inheriting a hospital three million dollars in the red, he put in place a program that turned the loss into a twelve million dollar gain a year later and a twenty-five million dollar bottom line the next year.

In addition, his leadership has resulted in a sharp change in market share—from 42 percent when he arrived to above fifty percent.

To Jason, however, financial performance and market share are secondary. He believes better results are a byproduct of the Radical Loving Care approach.

When you improve employee morale "remove the bad eggs" from leadership and strengthen patient satisfaction financial performance tends to improve, he says. Feature compassion as well as competence. This is Jason's recipe for success.

He hands out copies of *Radical Loving Care* to his staff. He also uses entries from our *Journal of Sacred Work* weblog as reflections to share with his staff.

In a remarkably short period of time, Jason Barker has led a transformation in culture. This has converted St. Vincent's into a true Healing Hospital

Scottsdale Healthcare System

One of the most unusual aspects of Radical Loving Care at **Scottsdale Healthcare System** is the level of physician involvement in the initiative. As a result of a staff-wide retreat and extensive follow-up addressing the impact of Radical Loving Care, the **medical staff leadership** decided to follow the example of The Cleveland Clinic and established the role of Chief Experience Officer.

This is the kind of follow-through that is crucial to making a difference. Interesting, also, is that they began with simple steps such as asking doctors to go up on the floors and thank the staff that looks after their patients. The effect, of course, was immediately positive and started momentum moving towards a new and richer culture.

Jan Jones

Some think that hospice organizations don't need to introduce Radical Loving Care because they already have a high standard of care. Experience shows otherwise. Every good hospice leader knows that significant improvement is crucial to consistently high-level care.

Consider the inspired hospice leadership of **Jan Jones** in Nashville and subsequently in San Diego.

Jan and her Executive Vice President, **Karen York**, introduced Radical Loving Care in 2005. Once again, it was the sustained effort to weave this work into the organization that deeply strengthened patient care.

None of these organizations is perfect, but all these efforts demonstrate that passing The Mother Test is necessary to the best patient care.

There are, of course, dozens of other hospitals, hospices and nursing homes where loving care is practiced at a high level. The problem is that they are still in the minority.

Too many healthcare organizations fail The Mother Test every day and night. This is both wrong and unnecessary.

Patients, by definition, are suffering. The suffering among us should never have to put up with anything less that the deepest kind of compassion matched with the highest competence.

Every patient is entitled to Radical Loving Care.

12

Further Strategies and Tools

Y ou can't learn things at a deep level by reading lists. But, once you have learned the core philosophy of loving care, lists can help as reminders that inform your work.

This is the thought behind the following summary.

Five Elements of Board Involvement

1. Involve the board members as soon as you are 1) clear on the concepts, and are 2) convinced that establishing a culture of loving care would help improve patient care.

2. The Board should establish a steering committee that supports the role of loving care as the core principle.

3. The Board should regularly assess how well the staff is doing in passing The Mother Test

4. Administrative leadership should regularly provide the board with reports on cultural initiatives.

5. Medical Staff should provide regular reports to the board on steps being taken to advance a culture of compassion among physicians

Seven Guidelines for Medical Staff Involvement

1) PLANNING: Share plans for culture change with medical staff leadership.

2) PLAN CREATION: Co-Create a plan for physician involvement.

3) LEADERSHIP: Identify a physician or physicians whose primary role is to develop, advance and recognize physician values around caregiving.

4) REWARD & DISCIPLINE: Doctors who advance compassion with competence need to be celebrated by both fellow physicians and first line caregivers. Provide levels of discipline for physicians who are disruptive.

5) GRAND ROUNDS: CME level programs focusing on the balance of compassion and competence need to be presented on a regular basis.

6) TRAINING ON ROUNDING: Physicians should mentor each other on compassionate care through rounding.

7) PRIVILEGES: The initial granting of privileges should include questions that ask physicians to state their commitment to compassionate care.

Ten Changes Leaders Can Make

Leaders set the example. Their first responsibility is to take care of the people who take care of people. Building a healing organization means that a culture of caring must pervade every activity.

Where attention goes, energy flows.

1. Hiring

Change it! Good teams start with good recruiting.

Don't be satisfied just to fill slots. If you want to strengthen your team, hire for a Servant's Heart. This also means retraining those who do the hiring so they know how to hire the best caregivers.

2. Orientation

Launch the IIF Strategy for New Employee Orientation

Orientations signal values to new employees. Most orientations are boring because they are nothing more than information dumps. Transform new employee orientation by using the IIF strategy that focuses on: *Information, Inspiration and Fun.*

3. Training

Move training beyond task performance.

Training should emphasize the balance of compassion with competence. Enrich staff teaching by focusing on the role of The Mother Test in leadership and in caregiving. Since we remember best what we teach, let students engage in teaching each other in addition to learning from the instructor.

4. Employee Reviews

Enhance the review process.

Key questions need to be added to monthly and annual reviews. Does the staff member display a Servant's Heart in his or her work? How does she or he give loving care?

5. Leadership Language

Positive language generates peak performance.

Negative language creates negative energy. Leaders need to engage the language of love, hope and affirmation. In a caregiving environment, positive language is the most effective. For example, instead of obsessing about mistakes, celebrate success.

6. Story Power

Storytelling is the biggest indicator of values.

Healing organizations tell stories that celebrate caregiving. Failed organizations try to avoid mistakes by terrorizing team members.

7. Meeting Agendas

Agendas signal priorities.

If leadership touts loving care but meeting agendas focus primarily on budget targets, then it's budgets, not caregiving, that matter.

8. Affirmation Rounding

Make rounding effective by focusing on encouraging and affirming.

This doesn't mean ignoring trouble. It means asking staff, "How do you give loving care?" It means thanking staff for their hard work focusing on those who are examples of that commitment. If staff members tense up when "the boss" comes around, then a culture of caring has not been established.

9. Supervisor Quality

The biggest determinant of patient satisfaction is employee satisfaction.

The biggest determinant of employee satisfaction lies in the leader to employee relationship. Employees don't need to love their boss. Bosses need to be tough-minded. But, they also need to be tender-hearted.

10. Rituals of Affirmation

Employee events are opportunities to strengthen cultures of caring.

Employee service award dinners are occasions to celebrate those who are living the values of the organization. Employees should be recognized for more than just years of service. Many healing organizations take rituals to a deeper level. One example is the "blessing of the hands" ceremony used in some Catholic hospitals.

About the Author

Erie Chapman has been called the father of the loving care movement in America. His nearly forty years' of experience as a hospital and healthcare CEO, nationally known speaker, lawyer, minister and bestselling author inform his universal message.

Across three decades Mr. Chapman served as President & CEO of Toledo's Riverside Hospital (now called St. Ann's) and Ohio's largest hospital, Riverside Methodist in Columbus. He is also the founding President & CEO of the ten-hospital U.S. Health Corporation (now called OhioHealth.)

Most recently, he served as President and CEO of Nashville's Baptist Hospital System and he is the founding President of The Baptist Healing Trust.

He has also had experience in the for-profit world as Chief Operating Officer of the publicly-traded InPhyNet Medical Management Company based in Fort Lauderdale.

In addition, Mr. Chapman is a former trial attorney, judge and television producer and host of the internationally syndicated show, "Life Choices with Erie Chapman" (1987-1995.) He is also an ordained minister and performs a ministry to prisoners on Tennessee's Death Row.

His first book, *Radical Loving Care*, became a best seller. His other two books are *Sacred Work, Planting Cultures of Radical Loving Care*, and *The Caregiver Meditations*.

As an artist, Erie is a prize-winning photographer and the award-winning producer and director of the documentary films "Acts of Caring," "Sacred Work," "The Servant's Heart," and "A Place Called Alive."

In addition, he has produced and directed two award winning feature films, "Who Loves Judas?" and "Alex Dreaming," and is a published poet.

Mr. Chapman has also composed the music for three CDs and for all of his films.

Dr. George Mikitarian, the veteran President & CEO of Florida's Parrish Medical Center says, "No one is doing more to affect the delivery of healthcare than is Erie Chapman."

Bestselling author David Whyte calls Chapman "a beacon of light in American health care." On the national ABC Special "Revolution at Work," host Forrest Sawyer reported that, "Erie Chapman created one of the most employee-friendly workplaces in America and [led] Riverside Methodist to be rated one of the top ten hospitals in the country." And Lloyd Dean, President & CEO of Dignity Health (formerly Catholic Health West) writes that, "Erie helps us understand that we need to be radical, loving, caring people who transform and heal our society."

A graduate of Northwestern University, George Washington University Law School, and Vanderbilt Divinity School, Mr. Chapman is currently President of Chapman Health International, Erie Chapman Foundation, and Dane Dakota Productions.

Erie's wife, Kirsten, is an award-winning journalist. They have two children and three grandchildren.

CPSIA information can be obtained
at www.ICGtesting.com
Printed in the USA
BVOW08s1109021117
499359BV00001B/39/P